ENERGY

TEAM GREEN SCIENCE PROJECTS

GREEN
SCIENCE
PROJECTS
ABOUT
SOLAR, WIND,
and
WATER POWER

Robert Gardner

E **Enslow Publishers, Inc.**
40 Industrial Road
Box 398
Berkeley Heights, NJ 07922
USA

http://www.enslow.com

ENERGY

GREEN Science Projects About Solar, Wind, and Water Power

Library of Congress Cataloging-in-Publication Data

Gardner, Robert, 1929–
   Energy : green science projects about solar, wind, and water power / by Robert Gardner.
      p. cm. — (Team green science projects)
   Includes bibliographical references and index.
   Summary: "Provides environmentally friendly 'green' science projects about energy"—
      Provided by publisher.
   ISBN 978-0-7660-3643-7
   1. Power (Mechanics)—Experiments—Juvenile literature. 2. Science projects—Juvenile
      literature. I. Title.
   TJ163.95.G365 2011
   621.042078—dc22

                                                                2009043927

Printed in the United States of America

102010 Lake Book Manufacturing, Inc., Melrose Park, IL

10 9 8 7 6 5 4 3 2 1

To Our Readers: We have done our best to make sure all Internet Addresses in this book were active and appropriate when we went to press. However, the author and the publisher have no control over and assume no liability for the material available on those Internet sites or on other Web sites they may link to. Any comments or suggestions can be sent by e-mail to comments@enslow.com or to the address on the back cover.

♻ Enslow Publishers, Inc., is committed to printing our books on recycled paper. The paper in every book contains 10% to 30% post-consumer waste (PCW). The cover board on the outside of each book contains 100% PCW. Our goal is to do our part to help young people and the environment too!

Illustration Credits: Jonathan Moreno, pp. 71, 85; Stephen Rountree (www.rountreegraphics.com), pp. 31, 32, 36, 38, 44, 56 (a), 66, 90, 103, 107, 112, 118; Tom LaBaff and Stephanie LaBaff, pp. 41, 58.

Photo Credits: Acme Design Company, p. 13; Alex Bartel/Photo Researchers, Inc., p. 34; Christopher Bernard/istockphoto.com, p. 122; PEKKA PARVIAINEN/Photo Researchers, Inc., p. 93; RickBL/istockphoto.com, p. 29; Shutterstock.com, pp. 1, 6, 7, 9, 35, 37, 47, 53, 56 (b), 73, 76.

Cover Photo: Shutterstock.com

Contents

Indicates experiments that offer ideas for science fair projects.

Chapter 4

Chapter 5

Indicates experiments that offer ideas for science fair projects.

Introduction

Heating, cooling, and lighting buildings; fueling cars, trucks, planes, and trains; operating home and business appliances—all these things need energy! In this book you will learn about energy. You will find out where it comes from, why we need to conserve it, and why we need to develop renewable sources—sources that can't be used up. Learning about energy can be fun when you make discoveries through experiments. Some of these experiments also offer ideas for science fair projects.

At times, as you do the experiments, demonstrations, and other activities in this book, you may need a partner to help you. It would be best to work with someone who enjoys experimenting as much as you do. In that way, you will both enjoy what you are doing. **If any safety issues or danger is involved in doing an experiment, you will be warned. In some cases, to avoid danger, you will be asked to work with an adult. Please do so.** We don't want you to take any chances that could lead to an injury.

Like any good scientist, you will find it useful to record your ideas, notes, data, and anything you can conclude from your investigations in a notebook. By doing so, you can keep track of the information you gather and the conclusions you reach. It will allow you to refer to things you have done and help you in doing other projects in the future.

Science Fairs

Some of the investigations in this book contain ideas you might use at a science fair. Those projects are indicated with a symbol (✓). However, judges at science fairs do not reward projects or experiments that are simply copied from a book. For example, a diagram of an electric turbine would not impress most judges; finding a unique way to measure solar or wind energy would be more likely to attract their attention.

Science fair judges tend to reward creative thought and imagination. It is difficult to be creative or imaginative unless you are really interested in your project. Therefore, try to choose an investigation that excites you. And before you jump into a project, consider, too, your own talents and the cost of the materials you will need.

If you decide to use an experiment or idea found in this book for a science fair, find ways to modify or extend it. This should not be difficult. As you carry out investigations, new ideas will come to mind. You will think of questions that experiments can answer. The experiments will make excellent science fair projects, particularly because the ideas are your own and are interesting to you.

If you decide to enter a science fair and have never done so, read some of the books listed in the Further Reading section. These books deal specifically with science fairs. They provide plenty of helpful hints and useful information. The books will help you avoid the pitfalls that sometimes trouble first-time entrants. You will learn how to prepare appealing reports that include charts and graphs, how to set up and display your work, how to present your project, and how to relate to judges and visitors.

Your Notebook

Your notebook, as any scientist will tell you, is a valuable possession. Use it to hold ideas you may have as you experiment, sketches you draw, calculations you make, and hypotheses you suggest. Your notes should include a description of every experiment you do, and the data it yields, such as voltages, currents, resistors, weights, and so on. You might also add photographs. Your notebook should also contain the results of your experiments, calculations, graphs you draw, and any conclusions you may be able to reach based on your results.

The Scientific Method

Scientists look at the world and try to understand how things work. They make careful observations and conduct research. Different areas of science use different approaches. Depending on the problem, one method is likely to be better than another. Designing a new medicine for heart disease, studying the spread of an invasive plant such as purple loosestrife, and finding evidence of water on Mars require different methods.

Despite the differences, all scientists use a similar general approach in doing experiments. It is called the scientific method. In most experiments, some or all of the following steps are used: observation of a problem, formulation of a question, making a hypothesis (a possible answer to the question), making a prediction (an if-then statement), designing and conducting an experiment, analyzing results, drawing conclusions, and accepting or rejecting the hypothesis. Scientists then share their findings by writing articles that are published.

You might wonder how to start an experiment. When you observe something, you may become curious and ask a question. Your question, which could arise from an earlier experiment or from reading, may be answered by a well-designed investigation. Once you have a question, you can make a hypothesis. Your hypothesis is a possible answer to the question. (As a simple example, if you heat some water, your hypothesis might be that the temperature of the water will increase.) Once you have a hypothesis, it is time to see if your hypothesis is true.

In most cases, you should do a controlled experiment. This means having two groups that are treated the same except for the one factor being tested. That factor is called a variable. For example, suppose your question is "Does color affect the absorption of solar energy?" You might use several identical thermometers. One thermometer would be covered by white paper. It would be called the control (no color). The other thermometers, covered with equal weights of colored paper, including black, would be called the experimental thermometers. All the thermometers should be treated the same except for the color covering them. All thermometers should be placed in the same sunlight at the same angle to the sun for the same length of time. The color of the paper covering the thermometers is the variable. It is the only difference among the thermometers.

During the experiment, you would collect data. You would observe and record the temperatures under the different colored papers at equal time intervals. By comparing the temperatures of the control and experimental thermometers, you might draw conclusions.

Safety First

Safety is essential when you do experiments. The following safety rules are well worth reading before you start any project.

1. Do any experiments or projects, whether from this book or of your own design, **under adult supervision**, such as of a science teacher or other knowledgeable adult.

2. Read all instructions carefully before proceeding with a project. If you have questions, check with your supervisor before going any further.

3. Maintain a serious attitude while conducting experiments. Fooling around can be dangerous to you and to others.

4. **Wear approved safety goggles** when you are working with a flame or chemicals, or while doing anything that might cause injury to your eyes.

5. Have a first aid kit nearby while you are experimenting.

6. Do not put your fingers or any object other than properly designed electrical connectors into electrical outlets.

7. Never let water droplets come in contact with a hot lightbulb.

8. Never experiment with household electricity.

9. Do not eat or drink while experimenting.

10. Always wear shoes, not sandals, while experimenting.

11. The liquid in some thermometers is mercury (a dense liquid metal). It is dangerous to touch mercury or breathe mercury vapor, and such thermometers have been banned in many states. When doing these experiments, use only non-mercury thermometers, such as those filled with alcohol. If you have a mercury thermometer in the house, **ask an adult** if it can be taken to a local thermometer exchange location.

Energy and Its Nonrenewable Sources

Since the beginning of the Industrial Revolution, around 1750, fossil fuels have supplied most of the world's energy. Fossil fuels (coal, oil, and natural gas) are the remains of plants and animals that lived millions of years ago. These organisms decomposed, under high pressures and temperatures, turning into the fuels we mine today. Coal is mostly carbon. (The chemical symbol for carbon is C). Oil and natural gas are hydrocarbons—compounds of hydrogen (H) and carbon (C). An example of a natural gas is methane. Its chemical formula is CH_4. Each molecule of methane contains one atom of carbon and four atoms of hydrogen. An example of one of the many liquid compounds obtained from oil is octane, C_8H_{18}. Octane is one of the hydrocarbons found in gasoline.

How many atoms of carbon and hydrogen are found in each molecule of octane?

Fossil fuels are nonrenewable sources of energy. Half of the world's fossil fuels have already been used up. It took millions of years for them to form. Once we use their energy, there is no way to get them back.

Many electric power plants burn fossil fuels to produce electricity. The engines in cars, trucks, planes, and trains burn fossil fuels in order to transport people and supplies. We heat buildings by burning fossil fuels. In industries, we use them to manufacture products such as plastic, medicines, clothing, synthetic rubber, and many others.

As the supply of coal, oil, and natural gas diminishes, the cost of these resources increases. But there is an even more serious concern about fossil fuels. The products of their burning pollute Earth's atmosphere. When these fuels burn, they produce carbon dioxide and soot. Some also produce oxides of sulfur and nitrogen. The sulfur and nitrogen oxides combine with water vapor to form acids, which fall to the ground as acid rain.

Carbon dioxide (CO_2) is a greenhouse gas, as are methane, nitrous oxide, sulfur hexafluoride, small amounts of hydrofluorocarbons, and trace amounts of a few other gases. Greenhouse gases are so named because they cause what is known as the greenhouse effect. A greenhouse is mostly glass. It allows sunlight to enter and warm the inside. The glass also reflects much of the infrared radiation (heat) produced inside, so it stays in the greenhouse. Like the greenhouse glass, greenhouse gases reflect heat (infrared radiation) back to Earth. Because more of Earth's

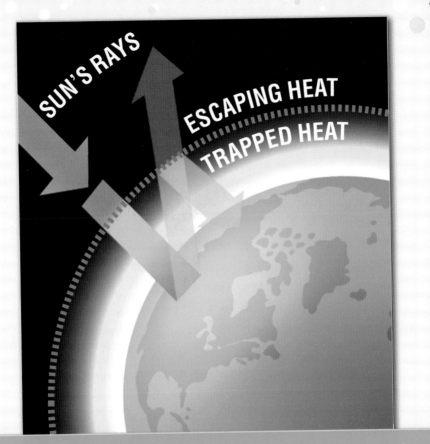

SUN'S RAYS

ESCAPING HEAT

TRAPPED HEAT

Like the clear ceiling of a greenhouse, certain gases in the atmosphere trap heat created by warming sunlight. The most abundant of the greenhouse gases is carbon dioxide. Greenhouse gases heat up a planet and cause global warming.

heat that would normally escape into space is being returned, Earth's temperature is slowly rising.

During the last 250 years, atmospheric carbon dioxide has increased dramatically. It has risen more than 40 percent, from 280 parts per million (ppm) to 390 ppm or more. This means that for every million molecules that make up air, 390 of them (0.039%) are carbon dioxide molecules. That percentage does not seem like very much. However, Earth's atmosphere contains more than five million trillion kilograms of primarily nitrogen and oxygen. And 0.039 percent of that atmosphere amounts to nearly two thousand trillion kilograms of CO_2.

Evidence of Global Warming

There is plenty of evidence that Earth is warming. Since 1900, Earth's average temperature has increased by 0.8°C (1.5°F). Its melting glaciers have shrunk by 5,000 cubic kilometers (1,200 cubic miles). Since 1980, scientists have recorded more than twenty of the warmest years on record. In the Northern Hemisphere, species of various animals are slowly advancing northward at a pace of four miles per decade. Mountain species are moving upland at twenty feet of altitude per decade. Springtime activities, such as the budding of plants, arrival of birds, and the end of frost, are advancing by two to three days per decade. Arctic winters are now 2.2°C (4°F) warmer than they were in 1970. The ice that covers the Arctic Ocean is shrinking. More than a million square kilometers (400,000 square miles) of that ice have disappeared since 1970—an area equal to that of Texas and California combined. Populations of polar bears and caribou—animals that live in very cold habitats—are decreasing. Earth's sea levels are rising because of the expansion of the warmer water and the melting of land glaciers.

1.1 Melting Glaciers and Sea Ice
(A Demonstration)

Things YOU will Need:

✓ 2 identical clear, tall, plastic cups or jars
✓ water
✓ 4 equal-sized ice cubes
✓ marking pen
✓ funnel

When the meltwater from land glaciers flows into the oceans, it raises the level of the sea. However, melting sea ice (frozen floating ocean water) does not affect sea level. To see why, carry out this demonstration.

1. Find two identical, clear, tall, plastic cups or jars. Add water to both until they are about half full. The water represents the oceans.

2. To one cup add two large ice cubes. These cubes represent the sea ice floating on cold oceans. Mark the water level in the cup or jar with a marking pen.

3. Place a funnel in the second cup or jar. Mark the water level. The marks on the two cups or jars represent sea levels.

4. Add two large ice cubes (equal in size to the two you added to the first cup) to the funnel. This ice represents the ice in land glaciers. The funnel's spout represents rivers leading to the ocean.

5. When all the ice has melted, look at the water levels in each cup or jar. In which has the water level risen?

Why won't melting sea ice raise the level of the oceans? If all the arctic sea ice were to melt, it would have no effect on sea level until it warmed and expanded. However, if the Greenland glaciers melted, it is estimated that sea level around the world would rise as much as 7 meters (23 feet).

What Is Energy?

Energy is not easily defined. It is not anything you can see or touch. But you can think of energy as something that enables us to get jobs done. It is what we need to move things, light lamps, heat buildings, and run household appliances.

Energy comes in many forms. Motion is one form. It is called kinetic energy. Another is thermal energy (heat), which is simply the motion (kinetic energy) of molecules. (Molecules move in all possible directions in a random manner. Therefore, the motion of molecules is often called random kinetic energy.) Temperature is a measure of the average kinetic energy of molecules. The faster the molecules move, the higher the temperature. Molecules of air have a faster average speed on a hot summer day than on a cold day in winter. We use thermometers to measure the temperature of air, water, and other substances.

Energy can be stored. Stored energy is called potential energy. A stretched spring, a raised weight, water at the top of a dam, and many chemical compounds have potential energy. The chemicals in fossil fuels and in a battery that can provide electrical energy are examples of chemical potential energy.

Potential energy can be activated (released as kinetic energy) and used to get jobs done (to do work).

Work is one way to measure energy. Scientists have defined work as an equation. Work equals the force exerted on an object times the distance over which the force acts.

work = force x distance, or $w = f \times d$

If you pull a box across the floor, the work you do is equal to your pulling force times the distance you move the box. Suppose you pull parallel to the floor with a force of 50 pounds and move the box 10 feet. The work you do is:

50 pounds x 10 feet = 500 foot-pounds

However, if you push as hard as you can against a building, you do no work. Why? Because your force does not move anything, so $d = 0$ and $f \times 0 = 0$.

Although energy, in general, can't be defined, the various forms of energy can be. For example, the kinetic energy (KE) of an object is one half times its mass (m) times its velocity (v) squared (v^2).

$KE = \frac{1}{2}mv^2$

The gravitational potential energy (GPE) of a weight at a height above a floor is defined as the weight times the height.

GPE = weight x height

The potential energy of the weight equals the work done to lift it through a distance equal to its height above the floor. The force needed to lift the object is equal to its weight. The distance it moved is the height to which it was raised.

work = weight x height, or
work = force x distance lifted

Other forms of energy such as light, thermal, chemical, nuclear, and elastic potential energy can also be defined. These different kinds of energy can be changed from one form to another. A basketball with gravitational potential energy can fall. As it falls, Earth's gravity does work on it, and the ball gains kinetic energy. When it hits the floor, the ball is compressed like a spring. It acquires some elastic potential energy. As the ball becomes less compressed during rebound, it loses elastic potential energy and regains some of its kinetic energy. But as you know, the ball does not bounce back to its original height. It never regains all of its kinetic or potential energy. In all energy transfers, some thermal energy "rubs off." In the case of the basketball, friction within the ball and between the ball and the floor produces thermal energy. The kinetic energy of molecules in the ball and the floor increases. The ball and the floor become warmer. If the ball bounces to half its original height, half of its original potential energy has been changed to thermal energy.

Conservation of Energy

How do we know that half the ball's original potential energy was changed to thermal energy? We know this because thousands of experiments have confirmed the law of conservation of energy: *Energy is never created or destroyed.* Energy can be transformed or transferred, but it is never lost or gained.

People may ask you to conserve energy. They are really asking you to transform as little energy as possible to get jobs done. Change as little chemical energy as possible in fuel oil or natural gas to the thermal energy needed to keep your home warm.

Convert as little electrical energy as possible to light your home. Burn as little gasoline as possible to provide the kinetic energy needed to move your family's car from place to place.

When the words *conserve energy* appear in this book, they mean "convert as little energy as possible from one form to another to get a job done." By conserving fossil fuels, you reduce the greenhouse gases added to the atmosphere. Whenever you conserve energy, you reduce your energy bills, because energy is not free. We have to pay for electrical energy, gasoline, heating fuels, and any other form of energy we use to get jobs done.

Power

Power is work or energy divided by time. It is the rate of doing work.

$$\text{Power} = \frac{\text{work}}{\text{time}} = \frac{\text{force x distance}}{\text{time}} = \frac{\text{energy}}{\text{time}}$$

If we measure force in pounds, distance in feet, and time in seconds, then power equals foot-pounds per second.

As you may know, power is also measured in a unit called horsepower (hp). One horsepower equals 550 foot-pounds (ft-lbs). The unit was invented by James Watt (1736–1819) when horses were an important source of energy. Watt was a Scottish instrument maker who invented the first practical steam engine. He is responsible for measuring power in units larger than foot-pounds.

Watt harnessed a horse to a weight through a rope and pulley. He found the horse could raise a

150-pound weight about 3 feet, 8 inches (3.67 ft) in one second. Therefore, he defined one horsepower to be equal to 550 foot-pounds per second because:

3.67 ft/s x 150 lbs = 550 ft-lbs/s.

Science honored Watt by naming a unit of power for him. Watts (W) are commonly used to measure electrical energy. One horsepower (550 ft-lbs/s) is equal to 746 watts.

The power company that provides homes with electricity measures power in kilowatts (kW). A kilowatt is 1,000 watts, just as a kilogram is 1,000 grams. The electric energy the power company provides is measured in kilowatt-hours, which is power times time. The following example will show you how this works.

If a 100-W lightbulb is on for one hour, the power provided to the bulb is 0.1 kW.

The energy to light that bulb for one hour is 0.1 kW-h because:

energy = power x time = 0.1 kW x 1 h = 0.1 kW-h

If the power company charges 10 cents per kilowatt-hour, it will cost one cent to operate the bulb for one hour.

0.1 kW-h x 10¢/ kW-h = 1¢

1.2 How Powerful Are You?

(An Experiment)

Things YOU will Need:
- bathroom scale
- pen or pencil
- notebook
- staircase or several staircases
- measuring tape or ruler
- a partner
- stopwatch

Do you think you are as powerful as a horse? Form a hypothesis. Then find out by doing this experiment.

1. Stand on a bathroom scale. How much do you weigh? Record your weight, in pounds, in your notebook.

2. Find a staircase or several staircases in a multifloor building. The longer the staircase, the better. Measure the vertical distance from the bottom of the first step to the top of the last step (for example, the height of the second floor above the first floor). You could also measure the height of one step and multiply that height by the number of steps. Or you may be able to measure the distance between two or more floors with a sturdy tape measure.

3. Stand at the bottom of the staircase. Have a partner with a stopwatch yell "go" as he or she starts the stopwatch.

4. When you hear "go," begin climbing the stairs as fast as you can. When you reach the top, your partner will stop the stopwatch.

5. Record the time, in seconds, for you to go up the stairs.

How much work did you do? How much power did you exert in foot-pounds per second? What was your horse-power? Was your hypothesis correct?

For example, suppose you weigh 100 pounds and you ran up stairs with a vertical height of 10 feet in 5.0 seconds.

The work done was:

100 lbs x 10 feet = 1,000 ft-lbs.

The power expended was:

1,000 ft-lbs/5 s = 200 ft-lbs/s.

The power in horsepower was:

$$\frac{200 \text{ ft-lbs/s}}{550 \text{ ft-lbs/s/hp}} = 0.36 \text{ hp (or about one-third as powerful as a horse).}$$

Ideas for Science Fair Projects

- Measure the power and horsepower of a number of different people. Can you find anyone as powerful as a horse? Do heavier people exert more power than lighter people? Are athletes more powerful than other people? Are athletes in one sport more powerful than those in other sports?

- Design and do an experiment of your own to measure people's horsepower.

- How does the length of time a person works affect his or her power? Do an experiment to find out.

Measuring Energy

Energy, like length, can be measured in various ways. You have read about foot-pounds and kilowatt-hours, and you have probably heard of calories (cal) and Calories (Cal). A calorie is the amount of thermal energy (heat) needed to raise the temperature of one gram of water one degree Celsius. A Calorie (with a capital C) is equal to 1,000 calories: it is the heat needed to raise the temperature of one kilogram (1,000 grams) of water one degree Celsius.

Energy engineers commonly measure energy in British thermal units (Btus). A Btu is the amount of thermal energy needed to raise the temperature of one pound of water one degree Fahrenheit. It is equal to 252 calories, or 0.252 Calorie.

Table 1 shows how to convert various energy units to Btus and vice versa. Table 2 (on the next page) shows how to convert the potential energy stored in various substances that burn into Btus. You will find this table useful later in this book.

Table 1: Converting from one energy unit to another.					
To convert units of	To units of	Multiply by	To convert units of	To units of	Multiply by
kW-h	Btu	3,412	Btu	kW-h	0.000293
Cal	Btu	3.96	Btu	Cal	0.252
joule	Btu	0.000952	Btu	joule	1,055
quad	Btu	10^{15}	Btu	quad	$1/10^{15}$

Table 2:
The potential energy, in Btus, stored in a number of combustible substances.

To convert the potential energy in	To Units of	Multiply by
1 gal of gasoline	Btu	124,000
1 ton of coal	Btu	26,200,000
1 barrel of crude oil	Btu	5,800,000
1 cord of wood	Btu	15,000,000
1 gal of #2 fuel oil	Btu	138.800
1 ft^3 of natural gas	Btu	1,028

Chapter 2

Solar Energy: A Renewable Energy Source

Fossil fuels account for more than 75 percent of all the energy used in the United States. About 12 percent comes from nuclear energy, and nearly 10 percent comes from renewable energy sources. In 1970, 95 percent of U.S. energy came from fossil fuels. The nation has made slow progress in becoming energy independent. We still import from other countries 70 percent of the oil used to produce gasoline, fuel oil, and other products.

Unlike fossil fuels, renewable sources of energy cannot be depleted. In this chapter we will focus on solar energy, which comes free in the form of sunlight. Other renewable energy sources, such as wind, geothermal, tidal, and ocean thermal, will be covered in Chapter 3.

Several other energy sources are also regarded as renewable, including biomass and trash. Energy from biomass involves the solar energy stored in plants. Plants use the energy in sunlight to convert carbon dioxide and water into the starches and sugars that make up plant tissues. The process is called photosynthesis. It is the basis for the growth of all green plants. (Photosynthesis removes carbon dioxide, a greenhouse gas, from the atmosphere, so planting trees is a sound way to combat global warming.)

Considerable quantities of alcohol have been produced by letting microorganisms act on biomass, such as corn. (The process is known as fermentation.) The alcohol produced is used to make gasohol, a mixture that is approximately 10 percent alcohol and 90 percent gasoline. Gasohol does reduce the amount of oil that must be imported from foreign sources. However, it is not a solution to global warming. Large amounts of energy are needed to convert corn to fuel. In fact, when all parts of the production and use of gasohol from corn are taken into account, they produce more greenhouse gases than the gasoline they replace. Furthermore, corn and sugarcane (another source of biofuel) are foods for both humans and animals. When they are used to make fuel, farmers must pay more for the grain to feed animals, which increases the price of meat. Growing more corn to produce alcohol decreases the land available for other crops and, again, increases the cost of other food.

Biomass other than corn and sugarcane includes wood chips, switchgrass, cornstalks, and other organic matter. All are renewable sources of energy. In the future, biofuels are likely to be made more efficiently. Enzymes made specially to break down the cellulose in plants not used for food will make compounds that can be fermented into fuels.

Many power companies burn trash to produce electricity. While there is probably no end to trash, burning it adds carbon dioxide to the atmosphere. And there are other problems. Energy is needed to collect and move the trash to the power plant. Many of the plastics produce poisonous gases when they burn. Some of the trash won't burn. It must be separated from the combustible trash, such as paper and wood. And energy is required to separate the metals for recycling.

Nuclear Energy

Nuclear energy can reduce our dependence on foreign oil, but it is not renewable. Some uranium or plutonium is changed to lighter elements when nuclear energy is used to generate electricity. A nuclear reactor contains uranium-235 atoms, one kind of uranium whose atoms can be split (fissioned) into lighter atoms. When this happens, there is a small loss of mass. The energy produced is equal to the loss of mass times the speed of light squared ($E = mc^2$). Since the speed of light is huge (300,000 km/s), these reactors provide plenty of thermal energy (heat). The heat is used to change water to the steam that turns the machines that generate electricity. While uranium is not renewable, there is enough to last centuries. However, there are dangers involved. In 1986, a nuclear reactor in Chernobyl, Ukraine, went out of control, releasing large quantities of radiation. Many people died of radiation poisoning, and the area became uninhabitable.

Greater danger lies in storing and transporting the reactors' radioactive waste. Much of the waste is stored underwater in numerous temporary sites around the world. It will be transported from these sites to permanent underground or undersea storage by truck, ship, or train. An accident could release dangerous radiation into the air. In the United States, there are only two permanent underground storage sites availvable—Yucca Mountain, Nevada, and Carlsbad, New Mexico. Many scientists believe the sites are not subject to earthquakes or flooding. However, residents near the sites are fearful of accidents and are resistant to the plan to bury radioactive waste near their homes.

Solar Energy

Sunlight is plentiful and costs nothing. It is also free of pollution. For many months in much of the world, the sun provides all the thermal energy (heat) people need to stay warm. At times, there is too much solar energy. Buildings have to be air-conditioned to be comfortable, and air-conditioning requires electrical energy.

If we could harness all the available solar energy, we would have much more energy than we need. The sun provides 1,370 watts per square meter to our outer atmosphere. Some solar energy is reflected into space. Some is absorbed by air and soil, which helps to keep Earth warm. The sun provides lots of energy that could be used to generate electricity and heat buildings. However, solar energy is spread over our entire surface and atmosphere, and it is available only during daytime. Clouds reflect sunlight, so less solar energy reaches the ground on cloudy days. For solar energy to provide energy at all times, there must be a way to store it.

One way to use this diffuse energy source is to concentrate the sunlight using mirrors or lenses. Experiment 2.1 will show you one way this can be done.

2.1 Concentrating Solar Energy
(An Experiment)

Things YOU will Need:

- an adult
- shaving or makeup mirror
- window with a view of some distant objects
- a partner
- sheet of white cardboard
- yardstick or meterstick
- bright sunlight
- convex lens, such as a magnifying glass

How do you think solar energy can be concentrated (brought together)? Form a hypothesis. Then do this experiment.

1. Obtain a shaving or makeup mirror. Feel its surface. Can you tell that its surface is concave like the inside of a saucer?

2. Hold the mirror close to your face. Look into it. You will see a magnified image of your face.

3. A concave mirror has a focal length—a distance from the mirror's surface where parallel light rays are brought together (concentrated). You can find the mirror's focal length. To do this, stand on the side of a room opposite a window that has a view of some distant objects. Hold the

mirror with its reflecting surface facing the window. Ask a partner to hold a sheet of white cardboard in front and slightly to one side of the mirror. Move the mirror and cardboard until a clear image of outside objects—such as trees or buildings—is seen on the cardboard (see Figure 1a).

4. Measure the distance between the mirror and the clear image on the cardboard screen. That distance is the focal length of the mirror.

5. Take the mirror outside. Hold the mirror so that it reflects bright sunlight onto the cardboard screen. **Do not look at the sun or at the reflected sunlight. It can damage your eyes.** What do you think you will see when the screen is one focal length from the mirror? Form a hypothesis.

Figure 1a

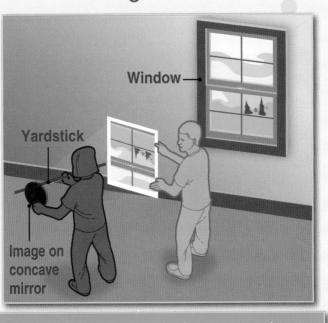

Finding the focal length of a concave mirror

Figure 1b

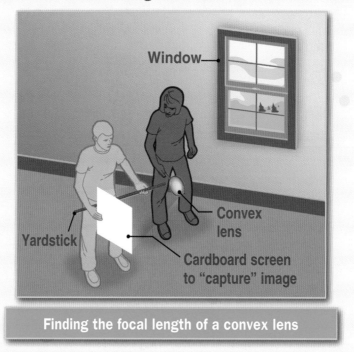

Window—

Convex
lens

Yardstick

Cardboard screen
to "capture" image

Finding the focal length of a convex lens

6. Check your hypothesis. **Under adult supervision**, move the cardboard so that it is one focal length from the mirror and in the path of the sunlight reflected from the mirror. Was your hypothesis correct?

What happens to the light on the cardboard if you move it farther from the mirror? Closer to the mirror?

Another way to concentrate solar energy is to refract (bend) sunlight. You can do this with a convex lens. A convex lens is thick in the middle and thinner around its edges. A magnifying glass is a convex lens.

7. A convex lens also has a focal length. To measure the focal length of the convex lens, you can use a method similar to the one you used to measure the mirror's focal length. This time the scene and the image of the scene are on opposite sides of the lens (see Figure 1b). The focal length is the distance from the lens to the clear image.

8. Take the lens outside. Under adult supervision, hold the lens so that it refracts (bends) bright sunlight onto a white cardboard screen. What do you think you will see when the screen is one focal length behind the lens? Form a hypothesis.

9. Check your hypothesis under adult supervision. Move the screen so that it is one focal length from the lens and in the path of the refracted sunlight that passed through the lens. Don't let the light stay on the cardboard for very long. It might start a fire. Was your hypothesis correct?

How could mirrors or lenses be used to produce the steam needed to turn an electric generator like those found in a power station? (Hint: Examine the photograph on the next page.)

Ideas for Science Fair Projects

○ Make a model to show why the images made by the concave mirror and convex lens were upside down.

○ The image of an object made by a concave mirror or a convex lens is right side up if the distance between object and mirror or lens is less than one focal length. Make a model to show why this is true.

The solar furnace at Odeillo, Font-Romeu, France, has sixty-three rectangular mirrors (foreground with red framework) that reflect sunlight onto the large concave mirror. The concave mirror focuses the sunlight onto a boiler, where steam is generated. The steam turns a turbine that generates electricity. The mirrors turn with the sun, so they reflect light onto the concave mirror throughout the day.

Air warmed by this solar collector provides most of the family's hot water needs.

Ways to Collect Solar Energy

One way to concentrate solar energy has been proposed by Cool Earth Solar in Livermore, California. Their plan is to use millions of large balloons made of plastic film. The upper half of the balloon would be transparent, allowing sunlight to enter. The lower half would be covered with a thin layer of aluminum. The aluminum would serve as a concave mirror like the one you used in Experiment 2.1. Light reflected by the aluminum would come together on a photovoltaic cell within the balloon. Photovoltaic cells can change light energy to electric energy. Wires would fasten the balloons to horizontal cables strung between vertical poles. These wires would also serve to carry electric current.

Rather than concentrating solar energy, we can let sunlight fall on a large area covered with photovoltaic cells. More and more homes and buildings are covering their roofs with photovoltaic cells. The electric energy produced can be used in the building. Any excess energy produced can be sold to the power company that provides the building with electricity.

Another method is to cover roofs with surfaces that absorb light and convert it to thermal energy (solar collectors). Buildings in the Northern Hemisphere that have south-facing roofs can use solar collectors to provide hot water and/or heat to keep the building warm in winter.

A solar collector (Figure 2) has a plate that absorbs solar energy. The plate is made of metal and painted black. A fluid (air or water) is passed over the plate. Heat is transferred from the plate to the fluid.

Figure 2

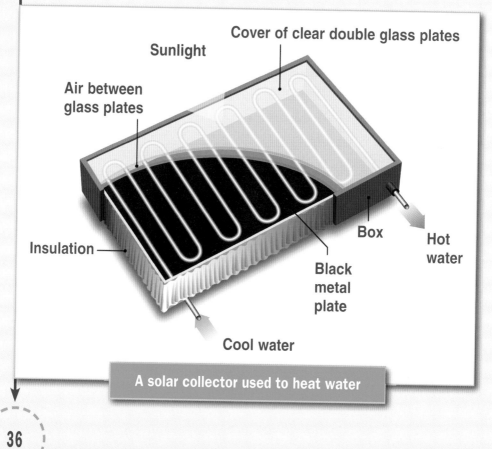

Sunlight

Cover of clear double glass plates

Air between glass plates

Insulation

Box

Hot water

Black metal plate

Cool water

A solar collector used to heat water

This home's south-facing roof is covered with solar collectors.

The fluid is circulated by a pump or fan. It transports the heat to the inside of the building. The collector is covered by two glass plates like a double-paned window. This makes the collector a miniature greenhouse. Sunlight passes through the glass. Much of its energy is absorbed by the dark metal plate. However, the glass does not allow much heat from the warm plate to escape from the collector. As a result, most of the heat produced by the sun is captured and transported to the inside of the building.

A similar greenhouse effect occurs when a car is parked in the sun. Even if it is cold outside, it will be warm in the car. The car's glass windows allow sunlight to enter and warm the car. However, the same windows reflect the warm but invisible infrared light

Figure 3

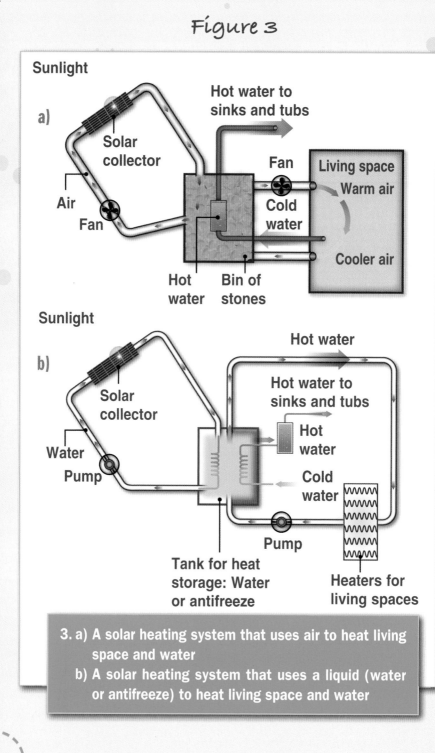

a) Sunlight
- Solar collector
- Air
- Fan
- Hot water to sinks and tubs
- Fan
- Cold water
- Living space
- Warm air
- Cooler air
- Hot water
- Bin of stones

b) Sunlight
- Solar collector
- Water
- Pump
- Hot water
- Hot water to sinks and tubs
- Hot water
- Cold water
- Pump
- Tank for heat storage: Water or antifreeze
- Heaters for living spaces

3. a) A solar heating system that uses air to heat living space and water
   b) A solar heating system that uses a liquid (water or antifreeze) to heat living space and water

released by the car's warm interior. As a result, initially more energy enters the car than leaves it.

Of course, the sun does not shine at night and is often behind clouds. To compensate for times of darkness and clouds, many systems store some of the heat. In air systems, this is done by circulating the hot air through a bin of stones (see Figure 3a). A tank to store hot water for household use may be embedded in the stones. The heat may also be stored in large tanks of water, as shown in Figure 3b. This system uses a liquid (water or antifreeze) to transfer heat.

In many areas, a backup system that heats with gas, oil, or electricity is available for prolonged periods without sunshine.

2.2 Light to Electricity
(An Experiment)

You will need a photovoltaic cell, an ammeter that can measure milliamperes, and two connecting wires.

1. When the sun is shining, take the photovoltaic cell, wires, and ammeter outside.

2. Use the alligator clips to connect the leads from the photovoltaic cell to the ammeter (see Figure 4).

3. Turn the photovoltaic cell toward the sun. What happens to the needle on the meter? If the needle turns the wrong way, reverse the connections to the meter. If the needle then goes off the scale, cover part of the photovoltaic cell.

4. How do you think the amount of photovoltaic cell surface exposed to the sun will affect the electric current? Form a hypothesis. Cover more and then less of the photovoltaic cell's surface exposed to the sun. Was your hypothesis correct?

Figure 4

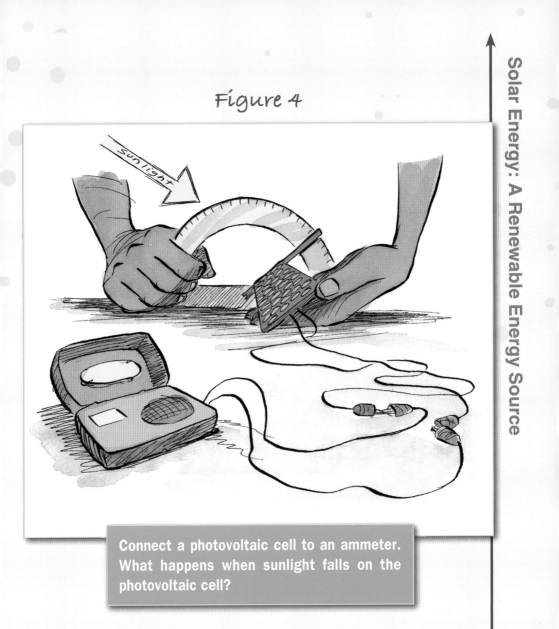

Connect a photovoltaic cell to an ammeter. What happens when sunlight falls on the photovoltaic cell?

5. How do you think the angle at which the sun strikes the cell will affect the electric current? Form a hypothesis. Then turn the cell to vary the angle at which the sunlight strikes the photovoltaic cell's surface. Was your hypothesis correct?

Ideas for Science Fair Projects

- Figure out a way to run a toy electric motor using photovoltaic cells.

- Does your home or school have a south-facing roof? If it does, investigate the cost of installing a photo-voltaic system that could provide some of the building's electrical energy.

Sun Power

To provide electrical energy to all of the United States using only solar energy would require a large area—one approximately 160 km (100 mi) on a side. This assumes photovoltaic cells will operate at 16 percent efficiency in the desert Southwest. There, six full-sun hours per day can be expected. To store enough energy to provide for a week's electricity with no solar output would require a large volume of batteries—about 1 cubic kilometer (0.22 cubic mile).

2.3 Sunlight to Heat in a Solar Collector (A Model)

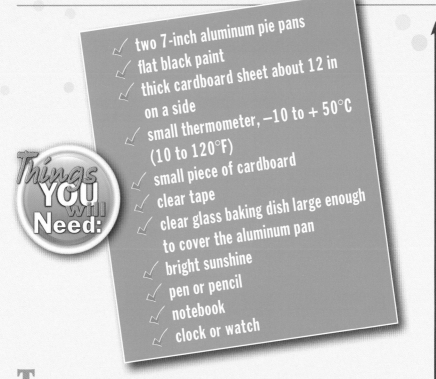

Things You will Need:

- ✓ two 7-inch aluminum pie pans
- ✓ flat black paint
- ✓ thick cardboard sheet about 12 in on a side
- ✓ small thermometer, −10 to + 50°C (10 to 120°F)
- ✓ small piece of cardboard
- ✓ clear tape
- ✓ clear glass baking dish large enough to cover the aluminum pan
- ✓ bright sunshine
- ✓ pen or pencil
- ✓ notebook
- ✓ clock or watch

To see how sunlight can be changed to heat, you can make a model of a solar collector that heats air.

1. Paint the inside of a 7-inch aluminum pie pan with flat black paint. This black pan can represent the surface of a solar collector that heats air.

2. After the paint dries, tape the pan, right side up, to a cardboard sheet. The cardboard will help to insulate the pan.

3. Use a small thermometer to determine the outside air temperature in the sun. Put the thermometer on the

Figure 5

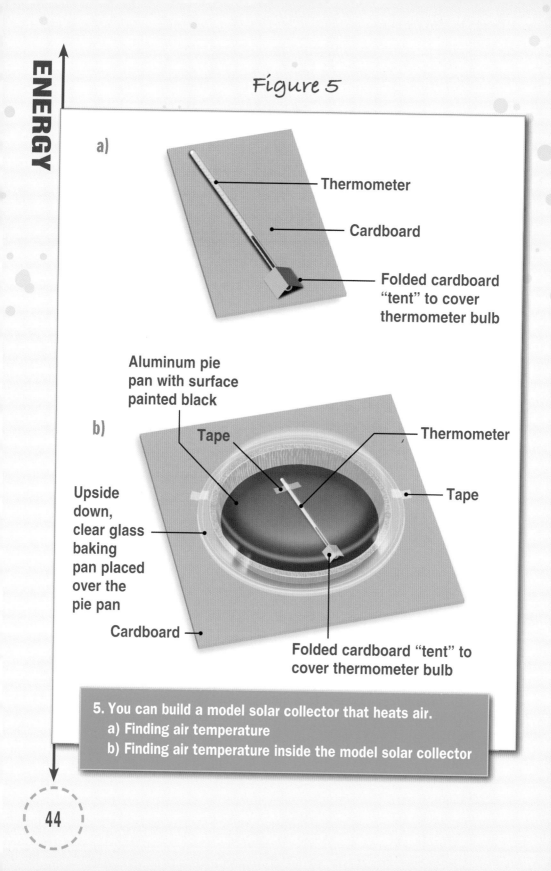

a)

Thermometer

Cardboard

Folded cardboard "tent" to cover thermometer bulb

Aluminum pie pan with surface painted black

b)

Tape

Thermometer

Tape

Upside down, clear glass baking pan placed over the pie pan

Cardboard

Folded cardboard "tent" to cover thermometer bulb

5. You can build a model solar collector that heats air.
   a) Finding air temperature
   b) Finding air temperature inside the model solar collector

cardboard sheet. Cover the thermometer bulb with a small folded piece of cardboard, as shown in Figure 5a. When the thermometer reading becomes steady, record the air temperature.

4. Put the thermometer with its shaded bulb in the black aluminum pan. Use a small piece of clear tape to fasten the thermometer to the pan (Figure 5b).

5. Cover the pan with a clear glass baking dish large enough to fit over the aluminum pan. The glass dish represents the glass cover over a solar collector. Tape the edges of the glass dish to the cardboard.

6. Place the cardboard sheet with its solar collector in bright sunshine. Lift and turn the cardboard so that the sun strikes perpendicularly (at 90°) to the model solar collector.

7. Record the temperature of the air in the solar collector at five-minute intervals. Keep recording until the temperature stops increasing. If the temperature gets close to the maximum the thermometer can measure, remove the glass cover.

What is the highest temperature you recorded? How does it compare with the air temperature?

8. To see how the black color affects a solar collector, find an identical unpainted pan. Repeat the experiment using the unpainted pan. What can you conclude?

Ideas for Science Fair Projects

- Design and do an experiment to find out how size affects a solar collector.

- Make a model solar collector through which water circulates.

- Design and build a model house heated with solar energy.

- Cover the thermometer bulbs of several thermometers with small sheets of construction paper, each of the same size but different in color. Place the thermometers on a cardboard sheet facing the sun. Which color is the best absorber of solar energy?

- Does the color of a building's roof affect the inside temperature of the building?

- The solar constant (1370 W/m^2) is the power the sun delivers to each square meter of Earth's atmosphere. This constant can also be expressed as 1.96 calories/cm^2/minute. Design and do an experiment to measure how much of the solar constant reaches Earth's surface on a clear sunny day and on a cloudy day.

- Design and build a solar heater that can be attached to a window and used to heat one room of your home. With parental permission, connect the heater to the room. How much will the heater reduce the energy and the money required to heat your home?

Passive Solar Energy

Solar systems, like the ones that were shown in Figure 3, use collectors to absorb energy, and pumps or fans to move the heated fluid around. Such systems are called active solar systems. Passive solar systems are different: they use no pumps or fans. A building with a passive system has a lot of south-facing windows to let sunlight in. The solar energy is absorbed and stored as heat in dark concrete walls and floors or by tanks of water. At night, insulated shades cover the windows. The warm concrete or water radiates heat to keep the building warm.

Some passive solar homes are partially buried. The temperature of soil is quite constant, and heat lost to cold infiltrating air is reduced. Fewer windows

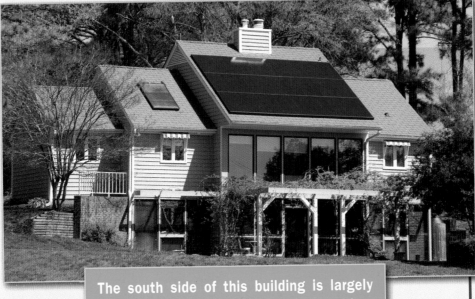

The south side of this building is largely glass. Passive solar heat can be stored in a thick concrete floor and water tanks.

on the north, east, and west sides of a building can also decrease heat loss.

A roof overhang can prevent light from the summer sun from entering a building. The sun's path across the sky changes from season to season. The sun is higher in the sky in summer than it is in winter.

2.4 Absorbing Solar Energy (An Experiment)

- an adult
- six identical metal cans
- flat black paint (spray can)
- water
- sand
- small stones or gravel
- salt
- soil (dirt)
- lead or copper BBs (optional, may be available at your school or from one of the science supply houses found in the appendix)
- one or more thermometers
- oven
- aluminum foil
- oven mitts
- cardboard
- clock or watch
- pen or pencil
- notebook
- bright sunlight

A passive solar system absorbs solar energy during the day. It radiates that energy to keep the building warm at night. In this experiment, you will test different materials. Which one or ones do you think will be the best to use to absorb and store solar energy in a passive solar building? Form a hypothesis. Then do the experiment.

1. Paint six identical cans with flat black paint.
2. When the paint is dry, fill the cans halfway according to the following data table.

Can Number	Fill with	Starting temperature	Final temperature
1	water		
2	sand		
3	small stones		
4	salt		
5	soil		
6	metal*		

DO NOT WRITE IN THIS BOOK

* For a metal, you could use lead or copper BBs, if available. If BBs are not available, can 6 may be excluded from the experiment.

3. Let the cans sit until their contents all reach the same temperature. Record that temperature as the starting temperature.

4. Place the cans side by side in bright sunlight for several hours.

5. After 2 to 3 hours, measure the temperature of the material in each can. Record the final temperatures in your data table. Which material reached the highest temperature?

The material that reached the highest temperature may not be the best one to use in a passive solar building. Some materials warm quickly because little heat is needed raise their temperature. Such materials will lose heat quickly as well. They would not be good solar energy absorbers.

Let's see which heat absorber can hold the most heat. This material will cool slowly.

6. **Under adult supervision**, place all the cans in an oven set at 150°F (65°C), or lower if possible. To prevent the water from evaporating, cover that can with aluminum foil.

7. After an hour, all the cans should be at the same temperature. To be sure that they are, put on oven mitts. Separately remove each can and record its temperature. Then put them back.

8. When you are satisfied that all the cans are at approximately the same temperature, remove them from the oven. Put them on a sheet of cardboard and remove the cover from the can of water.

9. Measure and record their temperatures every five minutes. Which material cools fastest? Slowest? Which material would be best for storing heat in a passive solar building?

Ideas for Science Fair Projects

○ Construct a model building with passive solar heating. Experiment with different materials to absorb and store heat.

○ What is the heat capacity of a sample of matter? How can you find the heat capacities of the materials you used in Experiment 2.4?

○ Repeat Experiment 2.4 using equal masses of the different materials rather than equal volumes.

Water, Wind, and Geothermal Energy

Electricity accounts for about one-third of all the energy used in the United States. It is a convenient energy because it can be carried by wires for long distances. Most of our electrical energy is produced by burning fossil fuels (coal, oil, and natural gas), which add to global warming. This is especially true of coal-burning power plants. U.S. power plants release more than 2 billion tons of carbon dioxide into the atmosphere each year. And coal is an inefficient way to produce electricity. Only about a third of the energy in the coal is converted to electricity. The rest is released as thermal energy (heat).

By using renewable energy sources (hydroelectric, wind, geothermal, and solar), we can reduce greenhouse gases. Consequently, the use of wind, water, and sun to generate electricity can reduce global warming. These alternative sources of energy could also help to reduce America's dependence on foreign oil. Some of the oil we import is used in power plants to generate electricity. Replacing these power plants with others that rely on renewable sources of energy will reduce our need to import oil.

One way to reduce the use of fossil fuels, and thereby, foreign oil imports, is to build more wind turbines. Wind turbines are similar to windmills. They have blades that turn in the wind. A shaft connected to the blades turns a generator that produces electrical energy. One proposal is to build wind farms along a corridor extending northward from Texas to Canada and westward from Texas to California. These regions provide consistent winds. Of course, a new and

These wind turbines are connected to a generator that creates electricity.

expensive electric grid would have to be built to carry electricity to other parts of the country. Since the wind doesn't always blow, batteries would be needed to store electrical energy that could be used when the air is still. Many believe vanadium batteries will allow adequate quantities of electrical energy to be stored.

In 2010, coal-burning power plants were providing 70 percent of the electricity in the United States. As the chemical equation below reveals, burning coal, which is mostly carbon, adds to global warming. Every pound of carbon in the coal that burns produces 3.67 pounds of carbon dioxide.

$$C \;+\; O_2 \;\rightarrow\; CO_2$$
carbon   oxygen   carbon dioxide

Most power plants produce electrical energy by burning fossil fuels to heat water, turning it into steam. The steam is used to turn giant turbines that spin electric generators. The generators, as you will see in Experiment 3.2, consist of wire coils that turn between magnets (magnetic fields). In hydroelectric plants, turbines are powered by water that spills over dams or waterfalls or that flows in rivers. Turbines can also be turned by tidal water, which ebbs and flows twice each day. They can be turned, too, by steam emerging from underground (geothermal energy).

Another renewable energy source is deep-ocean water (ocean thermal energy). There, turbines might be turned by pressurized gas with a low boiling point. Warm ocean water would be used to change the liquid to a gas.

The following demonstration will reveal what is needed to produce an electric current—a flow of electric charges.

3.1 A Simple Electric Generator

(A Demonstration)

A way to produce electricity without batteries was discovered by the great English scientist Michael Faraday (1791–1867). While experimenting with magnets and electricity, Faraday found that there is a magnetic field around a magnet. And he discovered a way to generate electricity using that magnetic field.

1. To see that there is a magnetic field around a magnet, move a magnetic compass around a bar magnet or several ceramic magnets stuck together. Notice how the compass needle points in different directions as you move

Figure 6

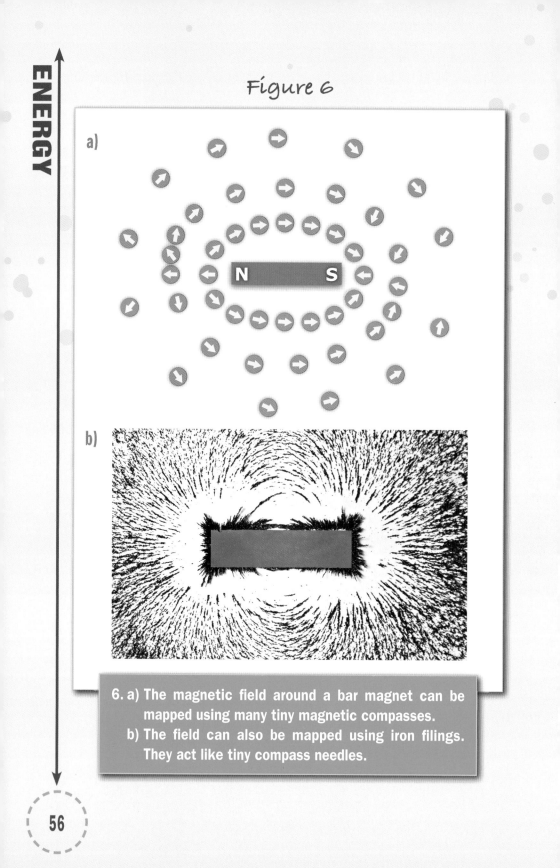

a) N S

6. a) The magnetic field around a bar magnet can be mapped using many tiny magnetic compasses.
b) The field can also be mapped using iron filings. They act like tiny compass needles.

it around the magnet. Faraday defined the direction of the magnetic field to be the direction that a compass needle points. By placing many tiny compass needles around a magnet, its magnetic field can be mapped (Figure 6a). Figure 6b shows how iron filings, which act like tiny compass needles, can also reveal the magnetic field around a bar magnet.

2. Earth has a magnetic field. Take a compass outside far from any magnetic material. Its needle will point in the direction of Earth's magnetic field, in a northerly direction.

   Faraday discovered a way to generate electricity using a magnet and wires. You can do something similar.

3. Make a simple meter that will respond to an electric current. Wind about 10 m (33 ft) of 24-gauge insulated wire around the outside of a roll of duct tape to make a coil, as shown in Figure 7a. Use some masking tape to keep the coils in place. Use a lump of clay to keep the coil upright and from rolling. Leave about 15 cm (6 in) of wire loose at each end of the coil.

4. **Ask an adult** to use sandpaper or a knife to remove about 2 cm (1 in) of insulation from each end of the wire.

5. Fold a strip of cardboard to form a platform. Put a magnetic compass on the platform at the center of the coil. The compass needle should point parallel to the plane of the coils, as shown.

6. Use two long insulated wires with alligator clips to briefly connect the two ends of the coil to a D cell. Simply touch the alligator clips to opposite ends of the D cell. What happens to the compass needle when electric current flows through the coil? As you can see, the compass needle acts as a meter showing when an electric current is passing through the coil.

Figure 7

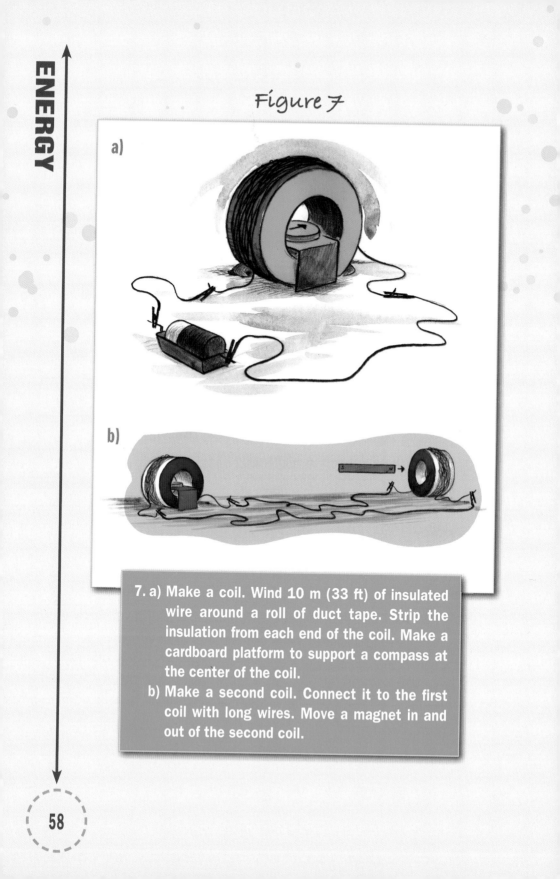

7. a) Make a coil. Wind 10 m (33 ft) of insulated wire around a roll of duct tape. Strip the insulation from each end of the coil. Make a cardboard platform to support a compass at the center of the coil.

b) Make a second coil. Connect it to the first coil with long wires. Move a magnet in and out of the second coil.

7. Build a second identical coil without the compass. The second coil should be far enough away from the meter (compass needle) so that a magnet has no effect on the meter.

8. Use the two long insulated wires to connect the ends of the two coils.

9. Move a strong bar magnet or a stack of six or more ceramic magnets in and out of the second coil (Figure 7b). How can you tell that an electric current is being generated?

   Does the compass needle move if the magnet is not moving?

10. To change the rate at which the magnetic field changes, move the magnet at different speeds. Does the rate at which the magnetic field changes affect the current that is induced?

11. Can you generate a current by moving the coil instead of the magnet?

Ideas for Science Fair Projects

○ Is the induced current you produced in Experiment 3.1 affected by the number of turns of wire in the coil? Do an experiment to find out.

○ Design and build an electric generator strong enough to light a flashlight bulb.

AC and DC

As you saw in Experiment 3.1, the compass needle moved one way as the magnet entered the coil and the opposite way when the magnet moved out of the coil. The needle movement shows that the electric current (moving charges) flows one way when the magnet is pushed into the coil and the other way when it is pulled out. This to-and-fro movement of the charges is called an alternating current (AC). Electric currents produced by batteries move in only one direction. This is called

Electrical Energy in Distant Lands

Many people who live in very rural parts of the world are far from electric power plants. They have no electric power. A company in California has developed a generator that can recharge 12-volt batteries, like the kind you find in cars. The generator is turned by pedals similar to those on a bicycle. Six hours of pedaling can generate enough energy to light six homes for a month.

A different approach has been proposed by Patrick Walsh, who founded the company Greenlight Planet. His lights are placed outdoors where they can be charged by solar energy during the day. At night they are brought inside to provide household lighting in homes that would otherwise be dark or in dim candlelight.

direct current (DC). The compass needle would be deflected only one way when connected to a battery.

Modern Generators in Power Stations

The generators in power plants are much larger and more complicated than the one you made. However, they are based on the same principle. Large coils, consisting of many turns of wire, rotate in a magnetic field. As the coil turns, the magnetic field through the coil is constantly changing. The changing field causes electric charges in the wires to move. The moving charges constitute an electric current. Wires conduct the charges to places far from the generator.

The electrical energy in your home or school is produced by giant AC generators in power stations. A rotator containing strong magnets fits inside giant coils of wire. In most commercial generators, the magnets rotate. These generators weigh hundreds of tons.

The rotors of the huge generators are turned by steam or water turbines. The steam may come from a solar or geothermal source, be generated by the heat produced when fossil fuels (coal, oil, or natural gas) are burned, or by the heat from a nuclear reactor. Water turbine blades are turned by moving water falling over a dam, flowing along a river, or flowing with the tide.

3.2 An Electric Motor as a Generator
(A Demonstration)

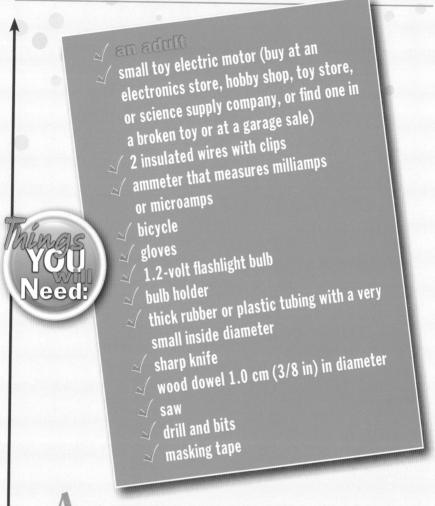

Things YOU will Need:

- ✓ an adult
- ✓ small toy electric motor (buy at an electronics store, hobby shop, toy store, or science supply company, or find one in a broken toy or at a garage sale)
- ✓ 2 insulated wires with clips
- ✓ ammeter that measures milliamps or microamps
- ✓ bicycle
- ✓ gloves
- ✓ 1.2-volt flashlight bulb
- ✓ bulb holder
- ✓ thick rubber or plastic tubing with a very small inside diameter
- ✓ sharp knife
- ✓ wood dowel 1.0 cm (3/8 in) in diameter
- ✓ saw
- ✓ drill and bits
- ✓ masking tape

An electric motor has one or more coils of wire that can turn between magnets. When connected to a battery, an electric current will flow through the coils. The magnetic field will push on the moving charges and make the coils turn. If, instead, the coils are turned, the magnetic field through the coils will change and electric charges will be pushed along the wires. The motor will become a small electric generator.

1. Examine a small electric motor. There should be two small metal leads outside the metal case. These leads are connected to the motor's coil. Use two insulated wires with alligator clips to connect the motor's two leads to the poles of an ammeter that measures milliamps or microamps. Electric currents (moving charges) are measured in units called amperes. (A milliamp is one thousandth of an ampere. A microamp is one millionth of an ampere.)

2. Spin the motor's shaft with your fingers. Is an electric current generated? What happens if you turn the shaft faster? What happens if you spin it in the opposite direction? How can you explain what you have seen?

3. Turn a bicycle upside down. You can use the bicycle wheel as a turbine to turn the generator's coils. Give the front wheel a good spin. Hold the ammeter connected to the generator (electric motor) while an adult, wearing a glove, holds the generator's shaft against the spinning tire. Can an electric current be generated by using the spinning wheel to turn the generator's shaft?

4. Connect the generator's leads to a 1.2-volt flashlight bulb in a bulb holder. Again, ask an adult, wearing a glove, to hold the motor's shaft against the side of a spinning bike tire. Can enough current be generated to light the bulb?

5. You may have to increase the friction between the spinning tire and the generator's shaft to make the generator's coils spin fast enough to light the bulb. To do this, slide thick rubber or plastic tubing with a small inside diameter over

the shaft. Cut it to the same length as the shaft. Or obtain a wood dowel with a 1.0-cm (3/8-in) diameter. Ask an adult to cut the dowel with a saw so that it is the same length as the generator's shaft. Then have the adult drill a hole through the center of the dowel that matches the diameter of the shaft. Push the dowel onto the shaft. If its diameter is slightly larger than the shaft, wrap a small piece of masking tape around the shaft. Then slide the dowel onto the shaft. The additional friction and diameter should enable you to light the 1.2-volt flashlight bulb.

Ideas for Science Fair Projects

- Figure out a way to generate a steady ongoing electric current from your small motor-generator.
- Build a demonstration to show how increasing the diameter of the generator's shaft affects its rate of rotation. Will it make the shaft spin faster or slower?

3.3 A Pinwheel Turbine
(A Demonstration)

In the previous experiment, you used a spinning bicycle tire as a turbine to turn a small generator. A toy pinwheel looks more like a turbine than a bicycle wheel does. Can the pinwheel turn the small generator (motor) you used in Experiment 3.2? Let's find out.

1. Because pinwheels differ, you will have to figure out a way to connect the pinwheel to the generator shaft. With help from **an adult**, you may be able to use a wood dowel, rubber or plastic tubing, and tape to make the connection. One example is shown in Figure 8a.

2. Use wires with alligator clips to connect the generator to a meter that measures milliamps or microamps. Use wind from a fast-spinning fan to turn the pinwheel turbine (Figure 8b). Does the generator produce an electric current when turned by a wind turbine?

Figure 8

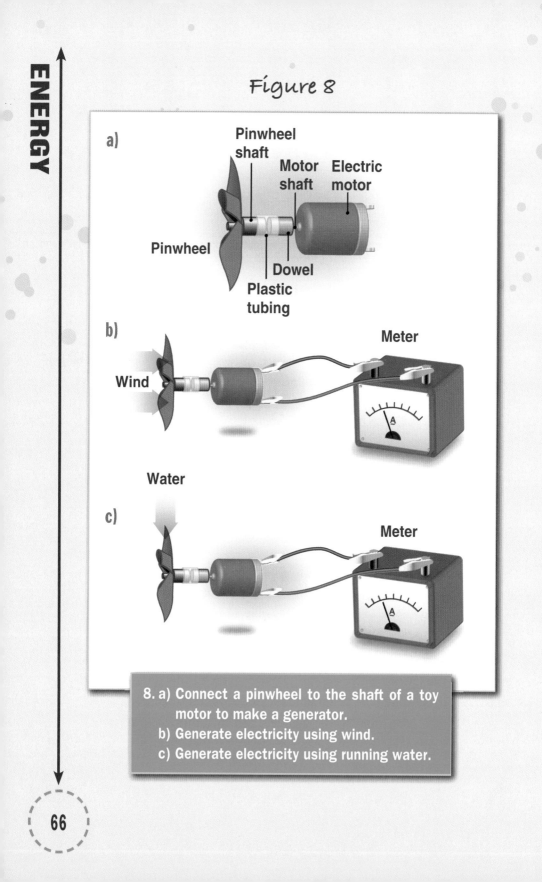

a)

Pinwheel
shaft

Motor
shaft

Electric
motor

Pinwheel

Dowel

Plastic
tubing

b)

Wind

Meter

Water

c)

Meter

8. a) Connect a pinwheel to the shaft of a toy motor to make a generator.
   b) Generate electricity using wind.
   c) Generate electricity using running water.

3. Use moving water to turn the turbine. Hold the pinwheel turbine in a stream of water from the cold-water tap in your kitchen sink (Figure 8c). Does the generator produce an electric current when turned by a water turbine?

Ideas for Science Fair Projects

- Under adult supervision, find a way to show that steam under pressure can turn a pinwheel turbine and generate electricity.

- Build a working model wind turbine of your own design.

- Make a model to show how electrical energy is transmitted from a power plant to homes.

Ocean Power

The ocean can provide electrical energy in two ways. The moon's gravitational pull on Earth causes high and low tides. High tides occur about every 12 hours and 25 minutes. The movement of tidal water can be used to turn turbines and generate electricity. Such power plants work best at the entrances to bays or estuaries, where dams can control the flow of tidal water. Unfortunately, there are few such places, and interfering with the natural flow of the water can affect the ecology of the area. A few tidal power plants have been built. One in France generates 240,000 kilowatts.

Another possible source of electrical energy is ocean thermal energy. In tropical ocean waters, the water at

F✓CT

Going "Green" to Make Snow

Making snow, running lifts, heating the lodge, and lighting the slopes at ski areas requires a lot of energy. To offset huge bills from power companies, the owner of the Jiminy Peak Mountain Resort in Hancock, Massachusetts, has installed a giant 386-foot wind turbine. By reducing his electrical costs, he can now make twice as much snow at half of what it cost him earlier.

You may soon see wind turbines on other mountains where skiers enjoy this winter sport.

the surface may be 27°C (80°F). Much deeper, denser water may be as cold as 4°C (40°F). The warm water could be used to heat a fluid with a low boiling point such as ammonia. The ammonia gas, under pressure, could turn a turbine. Deep, cold ocean water pumped to the surface could be used to condense the hot gas (change it to a liquid) after it has passed through the turbine. However, long underwater lines would have to carry the electricity to distant cities. Furthermore, long-term ecological effects of such power plants might be harmful.

Recently, research began on a system that would use ocean and river currents to generate electricity. The method uses metal rods that are made to vibrate by the current. The researchers claim the method will be less costly than either wind or solar energy.

3.4 The Effect of Temperature on Water Density
(An Experiment)

The density of any substance is its mass divided by its volume. For example, the density of copper is 8.9 grams per cubic centimeter (8.9 g/cm^3). How do you think the density of water will vary with temperature? Form a hypothesis. Then do this experiment.

1. Weigh a graduated cylinder or a plastic metric measuring cup. Record its mass in grams.

2. Add 100 mL or any convenient volume of water to the cylinder or measuring cup. A milliliter (mL) has the same volume as a cubic centimeter (cm^3).

3. Reweigh the water and cylinder or measuring cup. Record the mass in grams.

4. How can you find the mass of the water? Record its mass.

5. What is the density of the water in g/mL or g/cm^3? Record the water's density.

6. Weigh 50 or 100 pennies. Record their mass.

7. To find the volume of the pennies, add them to a known volume of water. The pennies will displace their own volume of water. What is the volume of the water and pennies? What is the volume of the pennies?

8. Calculate the density of the pennies.

   Pennies used to be made of copper (density = 8.9 g/cm^3). Are pennies still made of copper? How can you tell?

   As you have seen, pennies are more dense than water, and they sink in water.

9. Find the volume, in cubic centimeters (cm^3), of a rectangular or cubic wood block. Remember, the volume of such a block is equal to its length × width × height. What is the block's volume? Record its volume.

10. Weigh the block. What is its mass in grams? Record its mass.

11. Find the block's density. Record its density. Is the block more or less dense than water?

12. Put the wood block in a pan of water. Does it sink or float?

   From what you have seen, what can you say about whether an object will sink or float in water? What will happen to an object more dense than water if it is placed in water? To an object less dense than water?

To see why cold ocean water is found deeper than warm surface water, you can do another experiment.

13. Nearly fill a clear vial or small glass with cold tap water.

14. Place a drop of blue food coloring in another vial or small glass. Then nearly fill the vial or glass with hot tap water.

15. Fill an eyedropper with the hot colored water. Put the end of the dropper near the bottom of the vial that holds cold water. Slowly squeeze the hot water into the cold water, as shown in Figure 9. What happens? Can you explain what you see?

Figure 9

Adding hot water to cold water

16. Repeat the experiment, but this time color the cold water. Predict what will happen when you slowly squeeze the cold colored water into clear hot water. Try it! Were you right?

How does the density of cold water compare with the density of warm water? Was your hypothesis correct?

Ideas for Science Fair Projects

○ Use a sensitive balance to find the density of ice water and the density of hot water.

○ Find the density of water at different temperatures. Use your findings to make a graph of water's density versus its temperature.

Geothermal Energy

Earth's interior is hot. The heat comes from the decay of radioactive elements, such as uranium, and from friction as the rocky plates that make up Earth's crust grind against one another. In some places, the heat creates geysers (steam that spouts out of the ground). This steam can be used to turn turbines and generate electricity. Iceland generates all its electricity from five geothermal power plants and six hydroelectric plants. Electrical energy in Iceland is abundant and cheap. Iceland also uses geothermal energy to heat many of its buildings.

If the United States could extract all its geothermal energy to a depth of two miles, it could generate all its electricity for thousands of years. Unfortunately,

Steam created by underground geothermal energy can be used to create electricity.

knowing where to drill to reach geothermal sources is a challenge, and drilling is expensive. As research on geothermal energy increases, it may become a fast-growing source of electricity.

Heat pumps take advantage of the geothermal energy that keeps deep soil warm. They can take the heat from the soil and use it to heat buildings. Heat pumps work like refrigerators. A refrigerator uses a coolant to take heat from the food inside and transfer it to the air outside. Heat pumps can also work in reverse, like an air conditioner, and transfer summer heat to the cooler deep soil. Electrical energy is needed to pump the fluid and distribute hot and cold air. Consequently, heat pumps are not efficient in all parts of the country.

Conserving
Electrical Energy

Regardless of your electricity's source, you can reduce the amount generated by conserving it. If less electrical energy is used, less needs to be generated by power plants. For power plants that use fossil fuels, generating less energy will reduce the amount of carbon dioxide spewed into the atmosphere. Reducing carbon dioxide emissions will help to reduce global warming. Conserving electrical energy will also conserve your family's money. Using less energy earns smaller electric bills.

In many places, you can request that your energy come from green (renewable) energy sources. The request may increase your electric bill slightly. However, you will be playing a role in the battle to reduce greenhouse gases and global warming.

Many hydroelectric plants use dams to control the flow of water as it spins the plants' turbines.

Measuring Electrical Energy

As you read in Chapter 1, electric energy from power companies is measured in kilowatt-hours (kWh). The energy is produced in power plants by generators turned by giant turbines. The generators cause negative electric charges (electrons) to move along wires that lead to homes and buildings that use the energy. The charges can move through the wires in lights, toasters, hair dryers, and other appliances in your home. Circuit elements through which charges travel include lightbulbs, motors, heating elements in toasters, and other things that run on electricity.

Batteries also induce electrons to move. The electrons travel along a wire from the negative (–) pole of the battery to the positive (+) pole. A battery's positive pole is usually marked with a plus sign (+). The path the charges follow as they move from one pole of a battery or generator to the other is called a complete electric circuit. Unless the circuit is connected to both battery or generator poles, the circuit is not complete. Charges will not move unless there is a complete circuit.

You can think of electricity as bundles of electric charges. A bundle of charges, which contains 6,250,000,000,000,000,000 (6.25 million trillion) electrons, is called a coulomb (C). Electric current is the rate at which coulombs flow along wires. Electric current can be measured with a meter called an ammeter. Ammeters measure current in amperes. One ampere (A) is a current (charge flow) of one coulomb per second (C/s).

$$1.0 \text{ A} = 1.0 \text{ C/s}$$

Each coulomb carries electric energy. The energy carried per coulomb is called voltage. It can be measured with a voltmeter. Since voltage measures energy per charge, and current measures charge per time, we can find the power by multiplying the current times the voltage.

Voltage x current = power

Therefore,

$$\frac{\text{energy}}{\text{charge}} \times \frac{\text{charge}}{\text{time}} = \frac{\text{energy}}{\text{time}} = \text{power}.$$

Or, in units,

volts x amperes = watts.

The electrical energy carried by the electrical charges will be converted to heat, light, motion, or some other form of energy as it flows through circuit elements.

In the United States, most household electric circuits operate at about 120 volts. (Some circuits, such as electric stoves and clothes dryers, operate at 240 volts.)

If the electric current through a lightbulb is 0.5 A (0.5 C/s), the power provided to the bulb will be:

0.5 A x 120 V = 60 W or 0.060 kW,
since 1,000 W = 1.0 kW.

If the bulb is on for one hour, the energy provided to the bulb would be:

0.060 kW x 1 h = 0.060 kWh.

As you may know, a calorie is the heat needed to raise the temperature of one gram of water one degree Celsius. A kilowatt-hour is a sizable amount of energy. It can raise the temperature of 10 kg (10,000 g) of water, or about 2.75 gallons, by more than 86°C (155°F).

4.1 Power Ratings of Appliances

(Measurements)

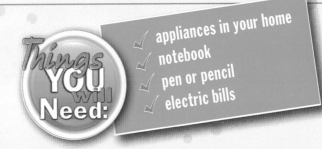

Table 3 lists some power ratings the author found on a few of the appliances in his home. The power rating written on an appliance provides the power in watts or kilowatts that will be supplied to the appliance when it is turned on. You may also find written on the appliance the current, in amperes (amps), that will flow through the appliance when it is turned on at a certain voltage, such as 120 volts.

1. Assume the cost of electricity is 10 cents per kilowatt-hour. How much will it cost to operate the appliances in Table 3 for one year? (Compare your answers with those on page 122.)

2. Find the power ratings on some appliances in your home. List them in a table.

3. Estimate the number of hours each appliance is used during a one-year period. Add those numbers to your table.

4. Ask a parent who pays the electric bill how much the power company charges per kilowatt-hour. Then calculate what it costs to operate each appliance for one year.

	Power Rating		Estimated use
Appliance	(Watts)	(kilowatts)	(hours per year)
coffee maker	850	0.850	360
lightbulb (incandescent)	100	0.10	100
lightbulb (compact fluorescent)	26	0.026	500
microwave oven	900	0.9	120
radio	6	0.006	900
television set	76	0.076	1,200
toaster	850	0.850	30
toaster oven	1,200	1.200	100

Table 3:
Power (wattage) ratings found on some appliances.

Which appliances cost the most to operate?

Which appliances could your family use less? By how many hours per year could their use be reduced? How much money could be saved by reducing their use?

The following section lists some things that might be done to reduce the use of electric energy in a home. Which of these things might you suggest to your parents to reduce their electric bill?

Ways to Reduce the Use of Electrical Energy from Power Companies

In the kitchen:

- Use an electric dishwasher only when it is full.

- Rinse dishes with cold water or in a pan of warm water. Don't use a stream of running hot water. It requires energy to heat water.

- Be sure your refrigerator door is well sealed. When closed, it should hold a piece of paper firmly.

- If you buy a freezer, buy a chest type. It loses less cold air when opened than an upright freezer.

- A freezer should be kept full to justify its cost. Buy food in quantity at sales and freeze. Fill space with jugs of water.

- When new appliances are needed, buy only energy-efficient ones.

- Electric stoves require a lot of energy. Therefore, if you cook with electricity:

  - cover pans when cooking.

  - be sure pans cover the heating element so that heat goes into the pans, not into the air.

  - cook as much as possible on heating elements; ovens and broilers use more energy.

  - when using the oven, cook as many foods as possible simultaneously in that oven.

  - turn off heating elements and ovens several minutes before food is thoroughly cooked; the hot elements and ovens will continue to heat the food and not the air.

In the laundry and bathroom:

- Wash clothes in cold or warm water. Rinse in cold water.
- Operate washers and dryers with full loads, but do not overload.
- Let dirty clothes soak before running the washer.
- Dryers use a lot of energy. They are on 240-volt circuits. Run no longer than necessary.
- Dry clothes on an outside line whenever possible.
- Wear wash-and-wear clothes to reduce the cost of ironing and dry cleaning.
- Insulate hot water pipes and older hot water heaters.
- Reduce the thermostat setting on your water heater to no more than 120°F.
- Turn off the water heater when you will be away for several days.
- Take quick showers rather than baths to reduce hot water use.

In other rooms:

- Turn off lights and other appliances such as radios and televisions when not being used.
- Keep lightbulbs and fixtures clean.
- Turn off outside lights when not needed.
- Use compact fluorescent bulbs rather than incandescent ones (see Experiment 4.3). Be sure they are Energy Star rated.
- Lower thermostats and wear sweaters. Turn thermostats back at night or when away, or install programmable thermostats that will adjust the heat for you.
- Do not leave computers, TVs, and video games in sleep or standby mode. Do not leave chargers plugged in when not in use. These devices continue to use electrical energy in those modes. Connect several of these items to a power strip that can be turned off.

Other ways:

- Install photovoltaic cells and/or solar heating panels on your roof.

- Encourage your town or city to build wind turbines on town-owned land and install photovoltaic cells on the roofs of town buildings.

- Ask your power company for an energy audit of your home. Most local power companies provide free audits.

- Make use of the sun when you read. Sit near a window so that you can read by sunlight rather than an electric light.

- Use a solar-powered battery charger to recharge batteries.

FACT

The television set in Table 3 is a 26-inch liquid crystal display (LCD) model. A similar size cathode-ray tube (CRT) TV is rated at about 100 watts. A 42-inch LCD operates at about 140 watts. A 60-inch LCD uses about 200 watts. Plasma TVs require significantly more energy than LCD TVs.

In 2008, the U.S. government encouraged greener TVs by awarding "Energy Star" labels to sets that are 30 percent more efficient than previous models. The U.S. Environmental Protection Agency (EPA) believes that if all TVs met Energy Star requirements, annual national household energy costs would decrease by a billion dollars, and reductions in greenhouse gas emissions would be equivalent to removing a million cars from highways.

4.2 An Immersion Heater and Wattage

(A Measurement)

Things YOU will Need:

Things YOU will Need:

- ✓ an adult
- ✓ immersion heater
- ✓ notebook
- ✓ pen or pencil
- ✓ ice cube
- ✓ glass
- ✓ kitchen sink
- ✓ thermometer (−20 to 50°C)
- ✓ graduated cylinder or metric measuring cup
- ✓ foam (insulated) cup
- ✓ electrical outlet
- ✓ watch or clock with second hand
- ✓ pocket calculator (optional)

Immersion heaters, like the one shown in Figure 10, have their wattage rating printed on them.

1. Record the heater's wattage. Also, make a note: 1 watt = 0.24 calorie/second (cal/s).

2. Put a thermometer near your kitchen sink. Wait several minutes to be sure the thermometer reading is steady. Record the temperature of the room.

Figure 10

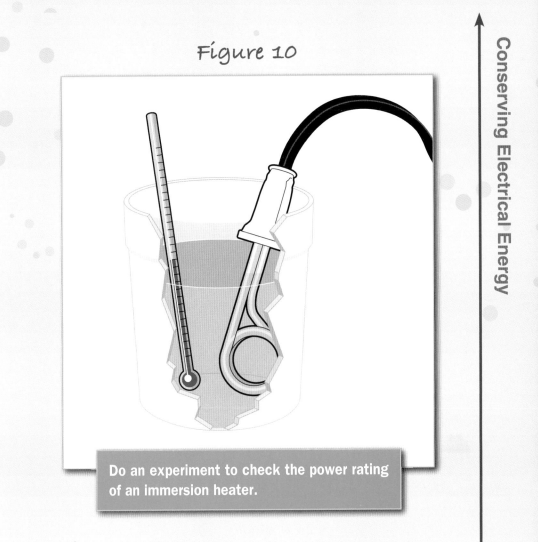

Do an experiment to check the power rating of an immersion heater.

3. Add an ice cube to a glass of water. Stir with a thermometer until the water temperature is about 8 to 10°C (14 to 18°F) below room temperature.

4. Pour 100 mL of the cold water into a graduated cylinder or metric measuring cup.

5. Pour the cold water into a foam (insulated) cup. A milliliter (mL) of water weighs one gram, so you are adding 100 g of water to the cup. Measure and record the temperature of the water.

6. Ask an adult to put the immersion heater into the cup of cool water while you hold the cup firmly in place.

7. Ask the adult to plug the heater into an electrical outlet and unplug it after exactly 30 seconds. Leave the heater in the water after it is unplugged. Heat remaining in the heater will be transferred to the water.

8. Stir the water with the thermometer until the temperature stops rising. Record the final temperature of the water.

How much heat, in calories, did the heater transfer to the water?

What is the wattage rating of the heater? How much heat, in calories, would you expect it to transfer to the water in 30 seconds? Remember, one watt is equal to 0.24 cal/s.

When the author did this experiment, he found the initial temperature of the cool water to be 15.5°C. After heating for 30 seconds, the water's temperature rose to 32°C.

The heat delivered to the water was:

100 g x (32.0°C – 15.5°C) = 100 g x 16.5°C = 1650 cal.

The power rating on his heater was 200 W, so the heater should have delivered

200 x 0.24 cal/s x 30 s = 1440 cal.

Since the heater delivered 210 calories more than expected, the author decided the power rating was not very accurate. It should probably have been rated at 230 W, since

**230 x 0.24 cal/s x 30 s = 1656 cal,
which is very close to 1650 calories.**

How much heat, in calories, did your heater transfer to the water?

Was the wattage rating of your heater accurate? If not, what do you think the rating should be?

Why did it make sense to cool the water a few degrees below room temperature before heating it?

Why was an insulated cup used? (Compare your answers with those on page 122.)

Idea for a Science Fair Project

Under adult supervision, use an immersion heater, foam cups, a timing device, a thermometer, and cold water to show that the amount of heat added to water is proportional to both the mass of the water and its change in temperature.

4.3 Fluorescent Versus Incandescent Lightbulbs
(An Experiment)

Things **YOU** will **Need:**

- ☑ incandescent lightbulb in fixture
- ☑ fluorescent lightbulb in fixture

Which do you think is more efficient, an incandescent lightbulb or a fluorescent lightbulb? Form a hypothesis. Then do this experiment.

1. Turn on an incandescent lightbulb and a fluorescent lightbulb that is about as bright as the incandescent bulb.

2. Hold your hand near, **not on**, the incandescent lightbulb. What do you feel?

3. Hold your hand near the fluorescent lightbulb. How does the fluorescent lightbulb differ from the incandescent lightbulb? Which lightbulb do you think is more efficient? Why?

Lightbulb Efficiencies

A lumen is the amount of visible light on an area of one square foot at a distance of one foot from a light source equivalent to the light from the flame of a certain candle. A light meter at this position would register one foot-candle.

The print on a package of 75-watt incandescent bulbs indicates that each lightbulb produces 1180 lumens. Its efficiency, in lumens per watt, would be:

$$\frac{1180 \text{ lumens}}{75 \text{ W}} = 15.7 \text{ lumens/W.}$$

A package of 18-watt compact fluorescent bulbs indicates that these lightbulbs provide 1100 lumens, almost as much light as the 75-watt incandescent lightbulb. The efficiency of these fluorescent lightbulbs is:

$$\frac{1100 \text{ lumens}}{18 \text{ W}} = 61.1 \text{ lumens/W.}$$

This indicates that fluorescent lightbulbs are nearly four times more efficient than incandescent light bulbs.

To show why incandescent lightbulbs are so inefficient, the author did an experiment. The apparatus he used is shown in Figure 11.

He cut four windows (openings) in a foam cup. He then placed a clear plastic sandwich bag in the cup and added 75 grams of water that he had cooled about 1.0°C below room temperature. He put a 6.3-volt flashlight bulb in the water and connected it to an ammeter and a voltmeter. He measured the water temperature with a thermometer that he could read to the nearest tenth of a degree Celsius. He then removed the thermometer, placed an insulated cover over the water, and submerged the bulb. He connected the circuit and let current flow for ten minutes.

Figure 11

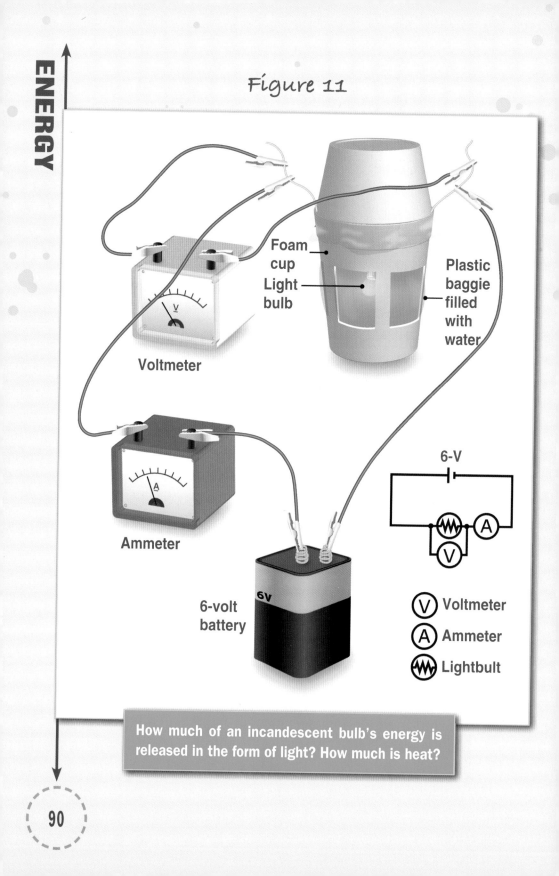

Foam cup

Light bulb

Plastic baggie filled with water

Voltmeter

Ammeter

6-V

6-volt battery

6V

(V) Voltmeter

(A) Ammeter

(M) Lightbult

How much of an incandescent bulb's energy is released in the form of light? How much is heat?

The current remained steady at 0.23 A. The voltmeter also remained steady at 5.4 V. Remember: voltage x current = power in watts, and 1 watt = 0.24 calorie/second.

After ten minutes, he disconnected the circuit, took the final water temperature, and examined his data, which is shown below.

Initial Temperature (°C)	Final Temperature (°C)	Voltage (V)	Current (A)	Watts	Time (sec)	Electrical Energy (cal)	Heat (cal)
19.5	21.0	5.4	0.23	1.24	600	180	150

The wattage for this experiment was:

5.4 V x 0.23 A = 1.24 watts.

The electrical energy provided in this experiment was:

1.24 x 0.24 cal/s x 600 s = 179 cal.
(Remember: 1 watt = 0.24 cal/s.)

That energy provided both the heat and the light.

The heat, in calories, was equal to the mass of the water times its change in temperature.

Heat = 100 g x 1.5°C = 150 cal

Most of the electrical energy (179 cal) was released as heat (150 cal). In fact, nearly 84 percent of the electrical energy was changed to heat. Only 17 percent of the electrical energy was transformed into light.

F✔CT

Light-Emitting Diodes

Light-emitting diodes (LEDs) produce light of a certain color. Different LEDs emit different colored light. White light can be produced by combining red, green, and blue diodes in one bulb. LEDs are twice as efficient as compact fluorescent bulbs, last eight times longer, and contain no mercury. LEDs have been used for colored digital and traffic signals for quite some time. However, producing price-competitive LEDs that emit a white light as strong as incandescent bulbs remains a challenge. But companies such as Lemnis Lighting and others are trying. With time and further research, LEDs may be the next generation of household lighting.

Ideas for Science Fair Projects

- Do an experiment to show that white light contains all the visible colors, from violet to red.

- Do an experiment to show that blue, green, and red lights can be combined to produce white light.

Heat

If you live where the winters are cold, your home has to be heated. Some of that heat can come from the sun or from electricity generated by wind power. But in many cases, the heat is provided by other sources—fuel oil, gas, or electricity from fossil fuels.

The farther north you live, the less solar energy you will receive in the winter. The sun will rise late and set early. It will also be lower in the sky. (See the photograph below.) Its light will pass through more atmosphere. More of it will be reflected or absorbed by air and other atmospheric particles. Its light will also strike Earth at an angle much less than 90 degrees, so it will be more spread out. More of the light will be reflected and still less heat will reach Earth.

In this chapter you will find ways to reduce the thermal energy (heat) needed to keep your home warm. By using less heat, you will conserve energy.

The sun's path across the sky in winter at about 42° latitude

5.1 A Basic Law About Heat
(A Demonstration)

Things YOU will Need:

✓ 48-oz (1.4-L) metal can
✓ 96-oz (2.7-L) metal can, pail, or cooking pan
✓ hot and cold tap water
✓ ice cubes
✓ 2 thermometers (−10 to 50°C or 14 to 120°F) that have the same temperature reading when placed in the same container of warm water
✓ notebook
✓ pen or pencil
✓ clock or watch

How does thermal energy (heat) move? You can do a demonstration to find out.

1. Half fill an empty 48-oz (1.4-L) metal can with cold tap water. Add ice cubes until the can is about two-thirds full. Stir the ice and water with a thermometer until the temperature is about 0°C (32°F). Then remove any remaining ice.

2. Add hot tap water to a 96-oz (2.7-L) metal can, pail, or cooking pan until it is about one-third full.

3. Put a thermometer in each can. When the temperatures stop falling or rising, record the temperature of the water in each can.

4. Put the can with the cold water into the container of hot water.

5. Measure the water temperature in both containers at one-minute intervals. Record those temperatures in a data table. Gently swirl the cold water can in the hot water between temperature readings. Continue recording until the temperature in both containers stops changing.

How did the final temperature of the water in the smaller can compare with the final temperature of the water in the bigger can or pan?

From this experiment, you can see that heat flows from matter at a higher temperature to matter at a lower temperature. It flows until the temperatures are equal.

Ideas for Science Fair Projects

● Repeat Experiment 5.1. This time put the cold water and ice in a smaller (16-oz or 0.5-L) metal can. Remove the ice after the temperature reaches 0°C (32°F). A smaller amount of cold water will be warmed by the same amount of hot water as before. Try to predict how the final water temperature in the two cans will compare with the final temperatures you found in Experiment 5.1.

● Repeat Experiment 5.1 once more. This time put the hot water in a 16-oz (0.5-L) metal can and the cold water in the 96-oz (2.7-L) can. Try to predict how the final temperature of the water in the two cans will compare with the final temperatures you found when cold water was in the 16-oz can.

Conduction of Heat

As you learned in Chapter 1, thermal energy (heat) is simply the random movement (kinetic energy) of molecules. In the winter, the air inside your home is warmer than the air outside. The walls, floors, and roof are in contact with colder air. The faster-moving molecules of the inside air bump into the walls, floors, and roof and transfer some kinetic energy to the slower-moving molecules and eventually to the cold-air molecules outside the home. In this way, heat is conducted from warm inside air to cold outside air.

Reducing heat conduction will conserve heat generated inside buildings. What can be done to reduce heat conduction? You can find out by doing some experiments.

5.2 Conduction of Heat
(An Experiment)

Things YOU will Need:

- ✓ wooden cutting board
- ✓ cloth towel
- ✓ metal pan
- ✓ freezer
- ✓ clock
- ✓ wooden bowl
- ✓ small metal cooking pan
- ✓ glass cooking pan
- ✓ hot and cold tap water
- ✓ large bucket or basin
- ✓ ruler
- ✓ ice
- ✓ 6- to 8-oz metal can
- ✓ thermometer (−10 to 50°C, or 14 to 120°F)
- ✓ 6- to 8-oz glass jar
- ✓ 6- to 8-oz foam cup
- ✓ graph paper
- ✓ pen or pencil
- ✓ notebook

What things do you think conduct (move) heat well and what things conduct heat poorly? Form a hypothesis. Then do this experiment.

1. In your kitchen, find a wooden cutting board, a cloth towel, and a metal pan.

2. Touch each of them. Does any one of the three feel colder than the others? Since they are all in the same air, can any one of the three really be colder? If not, how can you explain what you feel?

3. Put a metal pan and a wooden cutting board in a freezer. After twenty minutes, remove them from the freezer.

Hold one in each hand. How can you tell which material is the better conductor of heat? Which one conducts heat faster from your hand?

4. Fill a wooden bowl, such as a salad bowl, with hot tap water. Also, quickly fill a small metal cooking pan and a glass cooking pan with hot tap water.

5. Empty the wooden bowl and turn it over. Place your hand on the dry bottom of the bowl. Repeat the procedure for the metal and glass cooking pans. Which of the three solids best conducts (transmits) heat to your hand?

   Substances that conduct heat poorly are called thermal insulators. Substances that conduct heat well are called thermal conductors. Which of the substances you tested— wood, glass, or metal—would you call a thermal conductor? Which would you classify as a thermal insulator?

6. Do a more quantitative experiment (one using measurements). Fill a large bucket or basin to a depth of about 5 cm (2 in) with a mixture of ice and cold tap water.

7. Fill a metal can with hot tap water and measure its temperature. Put the can of hot water into the ice water. Record the temperature of the hot water every minute until it reaches 10°C (50°F).

8. Repeat the experiment using a glass jar with the same amount of hot water at about the same initial (starting) temperature.

9. Do the experiment a third time with the hot water in a foam cup.

10. Plot a graph of temperature versus time for each container. Plot all three on the same axes. Examine the three cooling curves. Which solid is the best conductor of heat? Which is the best insulator?

Ideas for Science Fair Projects

- Freeze some water in shallow plastic dishes or trays. Put some of the following objects on the ice: a stack of coins, a marble, a small block of wood, an eraser, a stack of metal washers, a stack of rubber washers, a plastic block, a piece of chalk. Which objects do you think will melt the ice and sink into it? Why? Which objects do you think will not sink into the ice? Why?

- Design and do an experiment to compare the rate at which the metals shown in Table 4 conduct heat.

Table 4:

The number of calories of heat (k) that pass through a cube 1 cm on a side in one second when the temperature on opposite sides of the cube differs by 1° C.

Substance	k	Substance	k
silver	0.97	mercury	0.020
copper	0.92	glass	0.0025
aluminum	0.50	water	0.0014
brass	0.26	wood	0.0005
iron	0.16	paper	0.0003
lead	0.08	felt	0.00004

5.3 Heat Flow From a House in Winter
(A Model)

Things YOU will Need:

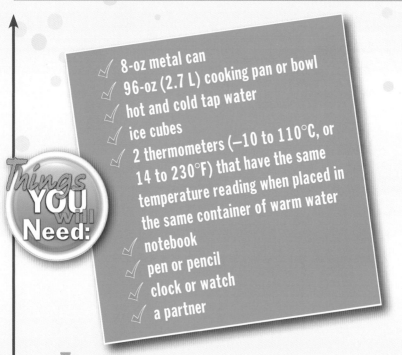

☑ 8-oz metal can
☑ 96-oz (2.7 L) cooking pan or bowl
☑ hot and cold tap water
☑ ice cubes
☑ 2 thermometers (−10 to 110°C, or 14 to 230°F) that have the same temperature reading when placed in the same container of warm water
☑ notebook
☑ pen or pencil
☑ clock or watch
☑ a partner

In winter, your house contains warm air. The huge volume of air outside is colder. Fluids are substances that can flow. Water and air are both fluids, so you can use a small amount of hot water to represent the warm air inside the house. Use a large amount of cold water to represent the cold air outside.

1. Add cold water to a large pan or bowl until it is about half full. Then add ice cubes and stir with a thermometer. Keep adding ice cubes and stirring until the temperature is about 5°C.

2. Add enough hot tap water to an 8-oz can so that the can rests on the bottom of the big pan or bowl. It should not float. Stir the hot water and record its temperature.

3. Continue to stir and record its temperature at one-minute intervals.

4. Ask a partner to continue adding ice cubes to the big pan and stirring to keep the temperature constant at about 5°C.

What happens to the temperature of the water in the small can? Does it reach the temperature of the water in the big pan? What would happen to the temperature inside your home in the winter if you turned off the heat?

5.4 What Can a Cooling Curve Tell Us?

(An Experiment)

- thermometer (−10 to 110°C, or 14 to 230°F)
- hot tap water
- graduated cylinder or metric measuring cup
- plastic cup
- pen or pencil
- notebook
- clock or watch with second hand
- graph paper
- Figure 12

Suppose a warm object is placed in cooler surroundings. How do you think the difference in temperature between them will affect the rate at which the warm object loses heat? Form a hypothesis. Then do this experiment to test your hypothesis.

1. Place a thermometer on the surface where you will do this experiment. Wait until the temperature is steady. Record the air temperature where you will do this experiment.

2. Into a graduated cylinder or metric measuring cup, pour 100 mL of hot tap water.

3. Pour the 100 mL of hot water into a plastic cup. Put a thermometer into the water and stir.

Figure 12

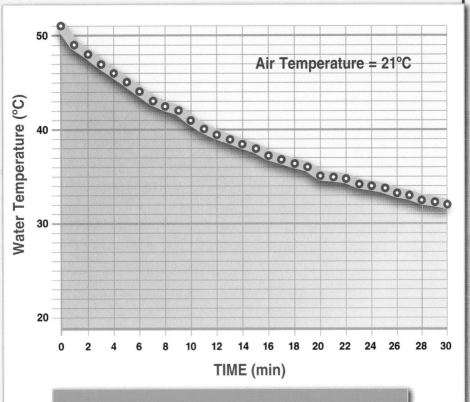

Air Temperature = 21°C

How does the temperature difference between an object and its surroundings affect the rate at which the object loses heat?

4. When the temperature is steady, record it in your notebook.

5. Stir the water and record its temperature at one-minute intervals for 30 minutes.

6. Use the data you collect to plot a graph of temperature, in degrees Celsius or Fahrenheit, versus time, in minutes.

7. Examine the graph carefully. How does the difference in temperature between the warm water and the cooler air affect the rate at which the water loses heat?

The author did this experiment in a room where the air temperature was 21°C. His results are shown on the graph in Figure 12. Is his graph similar to yours?

Notice that in the first three minutes of his graph the hot water's temperature fell 4.0°C, from 51°C to 47°C. It lost 400 calories (100 g x 4.0°C) to the cooler air. In the last three minutes of the graph, its temperature fell only 1.0°C. It lost only 100 calories to the cooler air.

Careful experiments show that the rate at which heat is lost to cooler surroundings is proportional to the temperature difference between them. Suppose the outside temperature is 40°F and the temperature in your house is 70°F. The temperature difference is 30°F. At night, you lower the house temperature to 55°F. Then the temperature difference will be only 15°F (55°F–40°F). The house will lose heat to the outside half as fast as it did before.

5.5 How Does Surface Area Affect the Rate of Heat Loss?
(An Experiment)

Things YOU will Need:

- ☑ an adult
- ☑ can opener
- ☑ 12-oz aluminum or steel can
- ☑ balance that can weigh to at least ± 1 g
- ☑ rectangular aluminum or steel pan about 8 in x 6 in
- ☑ aluminum foil
- ☑ hot tap water
- ☑ 2 thermometers (−10 to 50°C, or 14 to 120°F)
- ☑ pen or pencil
- ☑ notebook
- ☑ clock or watch
- ☑ metric ruler

Generally, a two-story house will have less surface exposed to the outside than a one-story house with the same amount of living area and type of construction. Is the rate of heat loss from such a one-story house greater than from a two-story house? How do you think surface area affects the rate at which heat is lost to cooler surroundings? Form a hypothesis. Then do this experiment.

1. **Ask an adult to help you** remove the top from a 12-oz metal can. Then weigh the can.

2. Also weigh a rectangular metal pan that is about 8 inches long and 6 inches wide.

3. If the pan and can are not about equal in weight, add some aluminum foil (or steel washers) to the lighter one until the weights are about equal.

4. Fill the can with hot tap water. Pour the water into the pan. Then refill the can with hot tap water. You now have equal volumes of hot water in the both the can and the pan.

5. Place a thermometer in both the can and the pan. Stir and record the temperature of the water in both the can and the pan.

6. Continue to measure and record the temperature in both the can and the pan at one-minute intervals for at least ten minutes.

Can you see, just by looking, that the water had more exposed surface area in the pan than in the can? If not, measure the surface areas, as shown in Figure 13. How does surface area affect the rate at which heat is lost to cooler surroundings? Was your hypothesis correct?

Convection: Another Way Heat Is Lost From Buildings

As you saw in Experiment 3.4, a warm fluid will rise in a cold sample of the same fluid. Movement of heat due to differences in the density of warm and cold fluids is called convection. Convection is one way thermal energy commonly moves in buildings. Air that

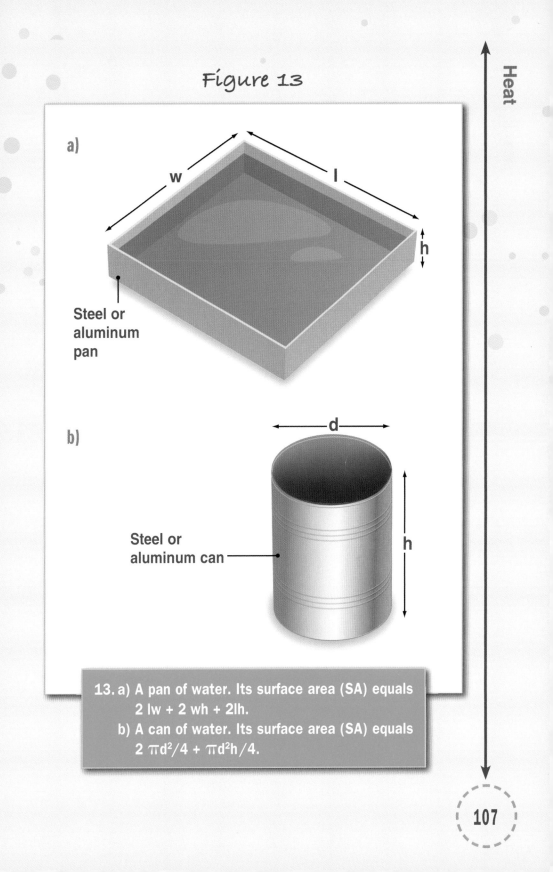

Figure 13

a)

w

l

h

Steel or
aluminum
pan

b)

d

h

Steel or
aluminum can

13. a) A pan of water. Its surface area (SA) equals
       2 lw + 2 wh + 2lh.
    b) A can of water. Its surface area (SA) equals
       2 πd²/4 + πd²h/4.

is warmed by a heater near a wall will rise and be replaced by cooler air near the floor.

Heat is also moved by convection currents caused by infiltration. Air leaking into buildings through cracks around windows, doors, and sills is called infiltration. This form of convection forces warm air out through other cracks. Heat losses resulting from infiltration must be replaced by the building's heating system. This is especially true when cold winter winds drive air through poorly caulked or poorly weather stripped doors and windows. Such energy losses can be easily eliminated or greatly reduced.

Ideas for Science Fair Projects

- Do an experiment to show that the rate at which heat is lost to cooler air is proportional to the surface area in contact with the cooler air.

- Use ice cubes with different surface areas, but equal volumes, to show how melting rate is related to surface area.

- Investigate ways in which the relationship between the rate of heat loss and surface area affects our lives— the way we dress, body parts that cool fastest, mittens versus gloves, and so on.

- Do experiments to show how wind affects the rate of heat loss to cooler surroundings.

5.6 Finding Infiltration
(A Measurement)

Things **YOU** Will Need:

✓ plastic wrap
✓ ruler
✓ tape
✓ pencil

You can make a simple instrument that will detect infiltration.

1. Cut a strip of plastic wrap about 15 cm x 8 cm (6 in x 3 in).

2. Tape a narrow end of the strip to a pencil.

3. Let the strip hang from the pencil. Blow gently on the instrument. What happens when moving air hits the strip?

4. Hold the instrument near windows and doors in your home that open to the outside. Can you detect any infiltration?

5. If you find that air is infiltrating around doors and windows in your home, tell your parents. Suggest that they buy weather stripping or caulk to seal these openings that let cold air into your home in the winter and out of your home in the summer. Weather stripping and caulk are not expensive, but they can greatly reduce heat losses and, therefore, heating bills.

6. Take your infiltration detecting instrument to school and look for infiltrating air there. Discuss your findings with a science teacher, custodian, or principal.

Radiation: More Heat Lost

Radiation is the transmission of energy, such as light energy, by electromagnetic waves. Unlike conduction and convection, radiation does not require matter for its transmission. It can travel through a vacuum. Standing in bright sunlight, you can feel the warmth from the sun's radiant energy. That energy was transmitted from the sun through empty space to Earth. You have probably felt radiant energy when you held your hands close to a fire or a lightbulb. You may have felt radiant energy leaving your body when you stood near a large, cold window. Radiant energy travels from warm bodies to cooler ones. If the walls, ceilings, and floors of your home are warm, very little thermal energy will be lost because of radiation. The major loss of heat from buildings is by conduction or convection. Relatively little heat is lost from buildings because of radiation.

Insulation

To reduce the rate at which heat is lost from a building, insulation (a poor conductor of heat) is placed in walls, above ceilings, and under floors. Some of the common types of insulation are mineral wool, chopped paper, expanded polyurethane, expanded polystyrene, and fiberglass. All are much better insulators than wood, concrete, brick, or glass.

These insulating materials are filled with small spaces that trap air. Air is a poor conductor of heat. Air molecules are relatively far apart, so they collide less often than solid and liquid molecules, which touch one another. By providing many tiny spaces that trap air, these insulators greatly reduce the flow of heat through a building's "skin" to the cold outside air.

Does the thickness of the insulation affect the rate at which heat is conducted? Let's find out.

5.7 How Will the Thickness of Insulation Affect Heat Flow?
(An Experiment)

Things YOU will Need:

- ✓ 4 or 6 seven-ounce foam cups
- ✓ scissors
- ✓ graduated cylinder or metric measuring cup
- ✓ hot tap water
- ✓ thermometer (−10 to 50°C, or 14 to 120°F)
- ✓ notebook
- ✓ pen or pencil
- ✓ clock or watch with second hand

How do you think the thickness of the insulation will affect heat flow through it? Form a hypothesis. Then do this experiment using cups made of foam, which is a good insulator.

1. Use scissors to cut off the top one-third of a foam cup. Set it aside. It will serve as a cover for another cup.

2. Into a graduated cylinder or metric measuring cup, pour 100 mL of hot tap water. Pour the hot water into a foam cup. Use a thermometer to measure the temperature of the hot water. Record that temperature.

Figure 14

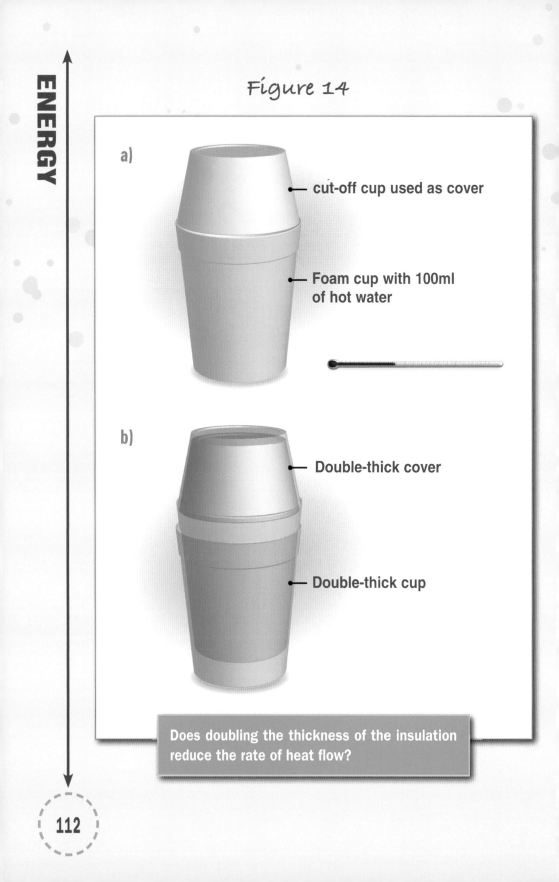

a) cut-off cup used as cover

Foam cup with 100ml of hot water

b) Double-thick cover

Double-thick cup

Does doubling the thickness of the insulation reduce the rate of heat flow?

3. Put the cover (the cup with the top cut off) on the foam cup that holds the hot water (see Figure 14a). Leave the cup covered for ten minutes, but swirl it gently every minute to keep the temperature uniform throughout the water.

4. After ten minutes, remove the cover and measure the water's temperature. How much did the temperature change? How much heat was lost?

5. Repeat the experiment, but this time double the thickness of the foam. To do this, put one foam cup in another (Figure 14b). Also, make a double-thick cover.

6. Pour 100 mL of the hot tap water into the double-thick foam cup. Measure and record the temperature. It should be about the same as it was at the beginning of the first experiment. Then proceed as you did with the single-thickness cup.

7. Examine the results of the two experiments. What do you conclude? Does increasing the thickness of the insulation reduce the rate of heat flow? Does it halve the rate?

Insulation and R-Values

Insulating materials are rated according to their ability to resist heat flow. A material's resistance to heat flow is known as its R-value. The R-values of various building materials are listed in Table 5.

As you probably discovered in Experiment 5.7, the thicker the insulation, the better its ability to reduce heat flow. In Table 5, you see that the R-value of a one-inch-thick layer of cellulose fiber (paper) is 3.7. A two-inch-thick layer of cellulose fiber would have an R-value of 7.4.

Table 5:
The R-values of various types of insulation and building materials.

Material	R-Value for one-inch-thick insulation	Material	R-Value for one-inch-thick insulation
INSULATION		**WINDOWS AND DOORS**	
Mineral wool batts	3.1	Single-glazed window	1.0
Glass fiber	2.2		
Rock wool	2.7	Double-glazed window	2.0
Cellulose fiber (paper)	3.7		
		Exterior door (wood)	2.0
Vermiculite	2.2		
Perlite	2.7	Exterior door (insulated metal)	15.0
Polyurethane (expanded)	5.9	**MASONRY**	
Polystyrene (expanded)	4.7	Concrete block (8 inches thick)	1.1
Polyisocyanurate sheathing	7.2	Concrete block (lightweight)	2.0
BUILDING MATERIALS		Brick, common (4 inches thick)	0.8
Wood sheathing (3/4 inch)	1.0	Concrete, poured (8 inches)	0.64
Plywood (1/2 inch)	0.63	**AIR FILM & SPACES**	
Bevel-lapped siding (1/2 inch)	0.81	Air space between building materials	0.9
Drywall (3/8-inch)	0.32	Air space between aluminum foil	2.17
Plywood panel (1/4 inch)	0.31		
Building paper	0.06	Air film on exterior surface	0.17
Vapor barrier (plastic)	0	Air film on interior surface	0.68
Wood shingles	0.97		
Asphalt shingles	0.44		
Linoleum	0.08		
Carpet + fiber pad	2.1		
Hardwood floor	0.71		

Notice that even the thin film of air that clings to both the inside and outside surfaces of a wall has an R-value. The outside film has a lower R-value because there is usually wind that tears away some of the air in the film.

Degree Days

How do fuel oil companies know when it is time to add fuel to their customers' tanks? They use degree-days to estimate fuel needs. But what is a degree-day?

Suppose today's average temperature is 55°F. To find today's degree-day value, you would subtract 55°F from 65°F, leaving you with 10°F. You would multiply 10°F by 1 day to obtain 10 degree-days. Any day with an average temperature at or above 65°F would have a value of zero degree-days.

Why choose 65°F as the basis for degree-days? Most homes do not have to be heated if the outside temperature is 65°F or higher. There is enough heat from other appliances—stoves, refrigerators, TVs, toasters, etc.—to keep the house warm.

As you saw in Experiment 5.4, the rate at which heat is lost to cooler surroundings is proportional to the temperature difference between them. If the average outside temperature today is 45°F, the heating requirement is 20 degree-days [(65°F – 45°F) x 1 day]. If yesterday's average temperature was 55°F—10 degree-days—the same house required only half as much heat to keep it warm. The total for the two days would be 30 degree-days. The total heating requirements for a year might be several thousand degree-days.

Table 6 provides approximate average annual degree-day information for a number of U.S. cities. A local fuel oil company can give you the number of degree-days for your community.

Table 6:
Annual degree-days for a number of United States cities.

City	Degree-days	City	Degree-days
Atlanta, GA	2,960	Chicago, IL	6,150
Boston, MA	5,630	Honolulu, HI	0
Detroit, MI	6,230	Portland, OR	4,630
New York, NY	4,870	Dallas, TX	2,360
Fairbanks, AK	14,280	Miami, FL	214
Pittsburgh, PA	5,985	St. Louis, MO	4,900

Calculating Heat Losses for an Entire Heating Season

From earlier experiments in this chapter, you know that heat loss from a building depends on several factors. Degree-days reveal the importance of time in measuring heat losses. You will use twice as much fuel to heat your home for two equally cold days as you would for one such day.

Heating engineers have a formula that allows them to estimate the total heat that will be lost (due to conduction) from a building during an entire year. You know that the heat lost from a building depends on its surface area, the temperature difference between inside and outside air, and time. Increases in surface area, temperature difference between inside and outside air, and time will all increase heat losses. However, insulation (R-values) will decrease heat losses. Taking all this into account, the formula for calculating the heat loss through any insulated surface is given below.

$$H = \frac{SA \times \Delta T \times t}{R}$$

In this formula, H is the heat lost, SA is the surface area, ΔT is the difference between inside and outside temperatures, t is the time the heat flows, and R is R-value.

Since annual degree-days (DD) takes into account both time and temperature difference for an entire heating season, we can modify this formula to find the heat losses for an entire year. That formula is:

$$H = \frac{SA \times 24 \times DD.}{R}$$

The 24 in this formula is the number of hours in a degree-day. It converts degree-days to degree-hours. This is necessary because R is measured in units of heat per hour, not per day.

Using this formula, we can calculate the total heat lost through a wall, floor, or ceiling for an entire year. Because of the units used for R, the formula will give you the heat lost in Btus (British thermal units), which you read about in Chapter 1 and Table 1. You may remember that a Btu is equal to the amount of heat

Figure 15

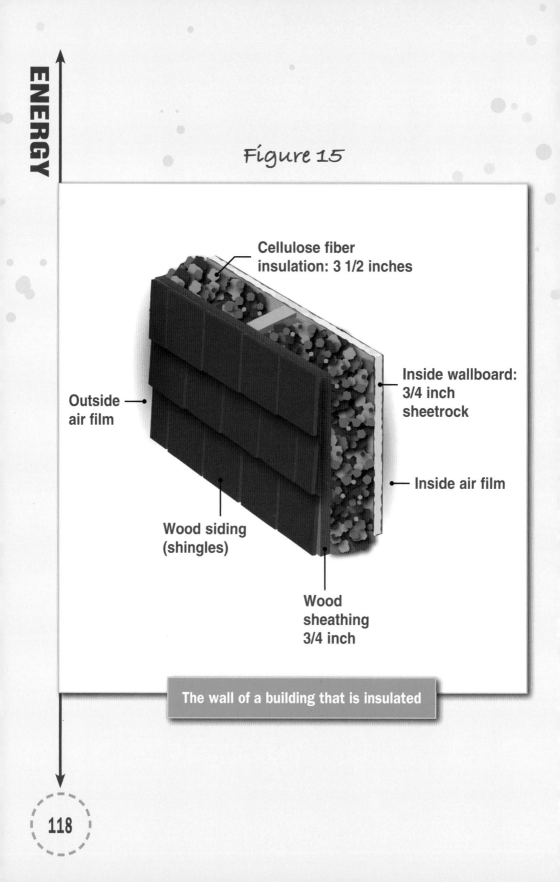

Cellulose fiber
insulation: 3 1/2 inches

Inside wallboard:
3/4 inch
sheetrock

Outside
air film

Inside air film

Wood siding
(shingles)

Wood
sheathing
3/4 inch

The wall of a building that is insulated

needed to raise the temperature of one pound of water by one degree Fahrenheit, which is equal to 252 calories.

Using this formula, we can calculate the total heat lost through a wall like the one shown in Figure 15. Let's assume the wall is one side of a house 20 feet high and 30 feet long. We begin by finding the total R-value for the wall (see Table 7).

Table 7: R-values for the wall in Figure 15.	
Material	R-value

Air films
    Outside
    Inside
	0.17
	0.68

Wood siding (shingles)	0.87
Wood sheathing	1.0
Cellulose insulation	12.95
Inside wall (drywall)	0.32
Total R-value	15.99

Let's assume the building is in Chicago, where the annual degree-days are 6,150. The area of the wall is 600 square feet (20 ft x 30 ft). Now we can find the total heat lost through the wall in one year using the formula from page 117.

$$H = \frac{SA \times 24 \times DD}{R} = \frac{600 \times 24 \times 6150}{15.99} = 5{,}538{,}000 \text{ Btus (rounded)}$$

Of course, we would have to find the heat lost through all the walls, floors, ceilings, and windows in order to determine the total heat lost due to conduction. Then we could calculate how much heating oil, gas, or electrical energy we would need to replace heat conducted from the building next year. As you know from the model in 5.3, any heat lost to the outside must be supplied inside if the building is to stay warm.

For the building in Chicago, just to keep the one wall warm would require 40 gallons of #2 fuel oil if the furnace were 100 percent efficient. We know this because Table 1 in Chapter 1 shows that one gallon of #2 fuel oil provides 138,800 Btus. Therefore,

$$\frac{5,538,000 \text{ Btus}}{138,800 \text{ Btus/gal}} = 40 \text{ gallons.}$$

If the building were heated by natural gas, 5,350 cubic feet would be needed, because:

$$\frac{5,538,000 \text{ Btus}}{1,028 \text{ Btus/ft}^3} = 5,387 \text{ cubic feet.}$$

If electric heat were used, 1,620 kW-h of electrical energy would be needed, because:

$$\frac{5,538,000 \text{ Btus}}{3,412 \text{ Btus/kW-h}} = 1,623 \text{ kW-h.}$$

Of course, we would also have to know how much heat is lost because of infiltration. Infiltration varies from building to building, but it too can be estimated.

Conserving Energy

- If you have a fireplace, be sure the damper is closed when the fireplace is not in use.
- If you have air-conditioning, set the thermostat at 78°F or higher during warm summer days.
- Be sure your water heater is insulated.
- Be sure windows have two panes or that storm windows are in place.
- Ask your school to start a "no engine idling" rule for vehicles waiting to pick up students.
- Turn off electric stove burners several minutes before food is fully cooked. The burners will remain hot long enough to finish the cooking.
- Run a second load when your clothes dryer is hot. It will save the energy needed to reheat the appliance.
- Caulk cracked, loose, or warped window frames and sills to prevent warm air from escaping and cold air from entering your living space through these uninsulated gaps.
- Special insulating covers are available for electrical outlets. They will stop cold air from entering your home's interior space.
- If you have a gas stove or furnace with a pilot light, be sure it burns with a blue flame. A yellow flame indicates poor efficiency and will release excess soot and carbon dioxide.
- If you burn wood in a fireplace, keep the fireplace in good repair. It will draw air better and burn wood more thoroughly. Be sure to use dry, seasoned wood. Green wood generates lots of smoke.
- Close the doors to unused rooms in your home and shut their heating vents. Money is saved for heat not used. However, be sure water pipes do not pass through rooms with temperatures that may be below freezing.

Answers

Experiment 4.1, p. 79:

Appliance								Cost
coffee maker	0.850	kW x 360 h x $ 0.10	=	$30.60
lightbulb (incandescent)	0.100	kW x 100 h x $ 0.10	=	$ 1.00
lightbulb (compact fluorescent)	0.026	kW x 500 h x $ 0.10	=	$ 1.30
radio	0.006	kW x 900 h x $ 0.10	=	$ 0.54
television	0.076	kW x1200 h x $ 0.10	=	$ 9.12
toaster	0.850	kW x 30 h x $ 0.10	=	$ 2.55
toaster oven	1.2	kW x 100 h x $ 0.10	=	$12.00
Total				**$57.11**

Experiment 4.2, p. 87:

- The water was cooled a few degrees below room temperature to compensate for heat lost to the air when the water was heated above room temperature. While the water was below room temperature, heat flowed into the water from the warmer air.

- An insulated cup was used to reduce heat lost or gained from the air.

Appendix:
Science Supply Companies

Arbor Scientific
P.O. Box 2750
Ann Arbor, MI 48106-2750
(800) 367-6695
www.arborsci.com

Carolina Biological Supply Co.
2700 York Road
Burlington, NC 27215-3398
(800) 334-5551
http://www.carolina.com

Connecticut Valley Biological Supply Co., Inc.
82 Valley Road, Box 326
Southampton, MA 01073
(800) 628-7748
http://www.ctvalleybio.com

Delta Education
P.O. Box 3000
80 Northwest Blvd
Nashua, NH 03061-3000
(800) 258-1302
customerservice@delta-
   education.com

Edmund Scientific's Scientifics
60 Pearce Avenue
Tonawanda, NY 14150-6711
(800) 728-6999
http://www.scientificsonline.com

Educational Innovations, Inc.
362 Main Avenue
Norwalk, CT 06851
(888) 912-7474
http://www.teachersource.com

Fisher Science Education
4500 Turnberry Drive
Hanover Park, IL 60133
(800) 955-1177
http://www.fishersci.com

Frey Scientific
100 Paragon Parkway
Mansfield, OH 44903
(800) 225-3739
http://www.freyscientific.com

Nasco-Fort Atkinson
P.O. Box 901
Fort Atkinson, WI 53538-0901
(800) 558-9595
http://www.enasco.com

Nasco-Modesto
P.O. Box 3837
Modesto, CA 95352-3837
(800) 558-9595
http://www.enasco.com

Sargent-Welch/VWR Scientific
P.O. Box 5229
Buffalo Grove, IL 60089-5229
(800) SAR-GENT
http://www.SargentWelch.com

Science Kit & Boreal Laboratories
777 East Park Drive
P.O. Box 5003
Tonawanda, NY 14150
(800) 828-7777
http://sciencekit.com

Wards Natural Science Establishment
P.O. Box 92912
Rochester, NY 14692-9012
(800) 962-2660
http://www.wardsci.com

Glossary

active solar systems—Systems that use pumps, fans, or other devices to move fluids heated by solar energy.

ammeter—A meter used to measure electric current in amperes.

ampere—A unit of electric current. One ampere (A) is a current (charge flow) of one coulomb per second.

biomass energy—The solar energy stored in plants.

coulomb—An electric charge consisting of 6.25 million trillion electrons.

density—The ratio of mass to volume for any given substance.

electric current—The rate at which coulombs flow along wires. It is measured in amperes.

energy—Something that enables us to get jobs done. It is sometimes defined as the ability to do work.

fossil fuels—Coal, oil, and natural gas, the remains of plants and animals that lived millions of years ago. These organisms decomposed under high pressures and temperatures, and became these fuels, which are mined today.

geothermal energy—Heat energy from Earth's interior. It may heat water that can be pumped to the surface, or that spouts out of the ground as geysers (steam).

global warming—The gradual warming of Earth caused by the greenhouse effect: an increase in greenhouse gases such as carbon dioxide, which traps heat energy near the surface.

gravitational potential energy—The weight of an object times its height above a surface to which it might fall.

greenhouse gases—Atmospheric gases that reflect radiant heat energy back to Earth.

joule—A unit of energy equal to 0.24 calorie, or the heat needed to raise the temperature of one gram of water 0.24°C.

kilowatt-hour—A unit used to measure electrical energy. It is equal to 3.6 million joules or 864,000 calories.

kinetic energy—The energy of motion, which equals one-half the mass of the moving object times its velocity squared ($1/2\ mv^2$).

nonrenewable sources of energy—Energy sources, such as fossil fuels, that cannot be replaced.

nuclear energy—The energy stored in the nuclei of atoms of elements such as uranium.

passive solar systems—Systems that absorb and store solar energy without the need for machines to move fluids.

potential energy—Stored energy, such as the energy stored in a stretched spring, a raised weight, and unstable chemical compounds.

power—Work or energy divided by time; the rate of doing work.

radiation—The transmission of energy, such as light, by electromagnetic waves.

renewable sources of energy—Energy sources such as wind, solar, tidal, geothermal, and ocean thermal that do not diminish with use.

thermal energy (heat)—The random kinetic energy of molecules.

volt—A unit used to measure electrical energy per charge. One volt is one joule per coulomb.

watt—A unit of power equal to one joule per second, or 1 volt x 1 ampere.

work—The force exerted on an object (in a direction parallel to the object's motion) times the distance that the force acts. Work = force x distance, or $W = f \times d$.

Further Reading

Books

Bardhan-Quallen, Sudipta. *Championship Science Fair Projects: 100 Sure-to-Win Experiments.* New York: Sterling, 2007.

Cherry, Lynne, and Gary Braasch. *How We Know What We Know About Our Changing Climate: Scientists and Kids Explore Global Warming.* Nevada City, Calif.: Dawn Publications, 2008.

Povey, Karen D. *Energy Alternatives.* Detroit: Thomson Gale, 2007.

Rhadigan, Joe, and Rain Newcomb. *Prize-Winning Science Fair Projects for Curious Kids.* New York: Lark Books, 2006.

Sobha, Geeta. *Green Technology: Earth-Friendly Innovations.* New York: Rosen Publishing Group, 2007.

Woodward, John. *Climate Change.* New York: DK Publishing, 2008.

Internet Addresses

Exploratorium: Science Snacks
<http://www.exploratorium.edu/snacks/iconheat.html>

Kids Saving Energy
<http://www.eere.energy.gov/kids>

Energy Kids
<http://tonto.eia.doe.gov/kids/>

Index